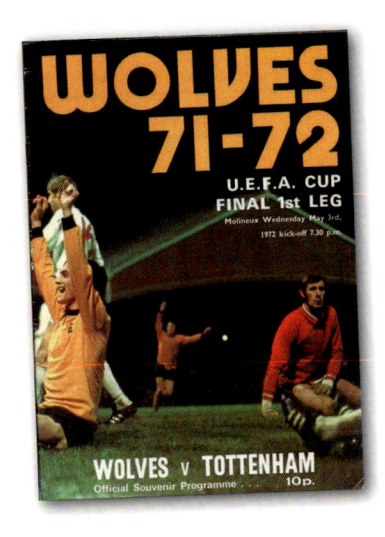

Conker Editions Ltd
22 Cosby Road
Littlethorpe
Leicester
LE19 2HF
Email: books@conkereditions.co.uk
Website: www.conkereditions.co.uk
First published by Conker Editions Ltd 2024.
Text © 2024 Steve Plant.

A CIP catalogue record for this book is available from the British Library.
13-digit ISBN: 9781739770587.
Design and typesetting by Gary Silke.
Printed in the UK by Mixam.

OLD GOLD AND BLACK

WOLVERHAMPTON WANDERERS: 'THEY WORE THE SHIRT'

STEVE PLANT

CONKER

In memory of my dad who inspired the 'They Wore the Shirt' project and my mom who we sadly lost in 2023.
I dedicate this book to every Wolves fan sadly no longer with us and hope that we continue to do them proud.

Foreword

What a pleasure it was to play in Wolves for six years, I cannot explain to you how much me and my family loved to be with you all. Today we still speak a lot about the club, even my kids have the best memories there and speak a lot about our house in Wolverhampton.

Without a doubt it was a beautiful journey – the first season was something special, the atmosphere, the way we played, the passion of the Championship...

The first Premier League season, it's difficult to say in words what we did and how we enjoyed. I think the confidence around the dressing room was special, we just didn't care about who we were playing, we just wanted to go on the pitch and show the Wolves team that we create together.

We achieved Europa League, European nights came to Molineux and what a shame it was to play the quarter-final away from our fans due to Covid. I truly believe if it was a normal time we could have done something even more special, everyone knows how hard it is to come to Molineux.

The last season was hard, problems that we hadn't faced before, fighting relegation is never easy but, again, this club is special in the right moments and together we did it.

The fans are special, I cannot describe the relationship we created. Since the very first day I just wanted to make them happy, and they made me feel at home since the Austria training camp when I joined the team.

The people in the city were so amazing with us, that was the biggest motivation for every season, to give them as much happiness as I could because they deserved it.

To be captain was the cherry on top of the cake, I was so proud, and at the end so relieved as well after that difficult season, maybe the hardest mentally of my career. To finish as captain and keep the team in the Premier League was the same feeling as being a champion!

The club just means so much to me and my family, I'm sure we will be back to see you all at Molineux.

And I can't wait for it...

Rúben Neves – May 2024

Introduction

Many of you will already know how my Wolves shirt collecting began from the two *They Wore the Shirt* books, but for those new to the story, here it is.

Football shirts had never really interested me until early in 2009 when we were told Dad had terminal cancer and could have as little as just three months left. He refused any treatment that could have given him a bit longer, and went downhill fast. Out of desperation we purchased a laptop for him to trace his family tree, to give him some interest. This helped to some degree but the breakthrough came when I purchased a George Elokobi shirt off eBay. Couple of holes, big Vick stain – turned out to be the

best £50 I have ever spent.

The interest Dad showed in the shirt encouraged me to build a website, the idea being I would add stuff to it every day and give him something to look forward to.

Anything and everything Wolves related quickly followed, and it worked so well that when we finally lost him in July 2012, it was a full three years after that bleak first prognosis.

He was proud of my collection and we had talked about me doing a book some day, so *They Wore the Shirt* followed four years later. We decided to give any profits to charity in Dad's memory, and after three books, several tribute dinners and other fundraisers, the total raised in his name now

stands at over £250,000.

The idea of this latest book is not only to update the previous editions, but also to make it more of a handy reference guide, and hopefully accessible to more fans. The first two were big, heavy coffee-table publications covering Wolves history in depth, whereas this one concentrates solely on the shirts.

For the first time, we've also included a section on replica shirts. Some of the older shirts from the late 1980s are as highly sought-after as the matchworn ones, and one Wolves shirt group on Facebook now boasts almost 8,000 members!

I've made some very good friends through this hobby and have been lucky enough to meet many of my Wolves heroes; but a special mention must go to Martin O'Neill. I won't go into how and why, suffice to say that he was not only a legend on the football field and in the dugout as a

top manager, but also as a person. My dad would have agreed, which is the highest compliment I can give.

Finally, a massive thank you to Rúben for the brilliant foreword, once a Wolf always a Wolf.

Steve Plant – August 2024

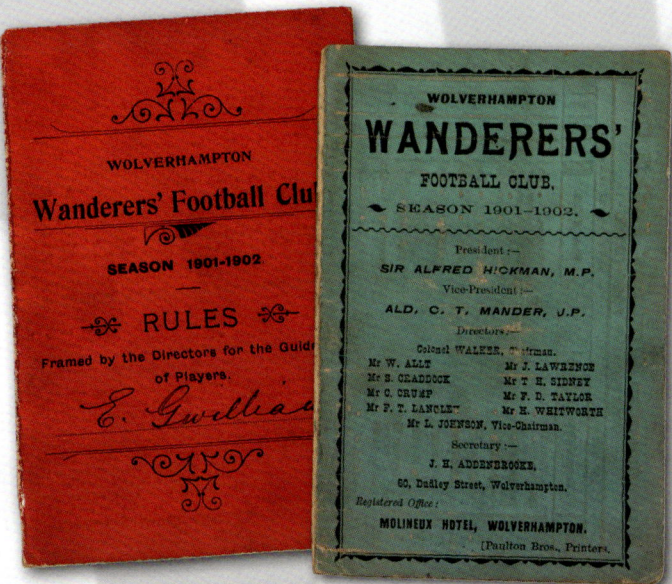

This is the oldest Wolves shirt yet to be found, and was worn in 1900. It has been proudly passed down through generations of Edward Gwilliam's family, along with his players' rule book and a

After wearing various coloured kits from 1877 to 1892, Wolves finally settled on Old Gold and Black as the club's colours. Diagonal half-and-half shirts were worn from 1892 to '93, but after beating Everton in the FA Cup final that season, decked out in gold and black stripes, the diagonal design was gone. This was the club's first major honour, and gold and black stripes of varying thickness remained a constant for the next 30 years.

letter from the club, dated 18th October, informing him that he had been chosen to play against Dudley at Molineux Grounds on Saturday, kick-off 3.15 pm.

This is the oldest shirt in my personal collection, and definitely has the strangest story of how it was obtained.

Found during a loft clearance in Alberta, Canada, it was originally thought to be an old ice-hockey jersey; however, 18 months of trawling the internet eventually led the owner to a black-and-white picture of the Wolves 1921 FA Cup final shirt, and his suspicions were first raised.

The club's co-founder Jack Brodie, who also played for Wolves in the 19th century, emigrated to Canada and it's believed to have belonged to his family.

Close examination of the shirt, including a comparison with an example from the same season in Molineux's museum, confirmed it was indeed one of the oldest shirts to survive from the club's

fascinating distant past.

Now buttons had given way to a lace-up collar; but perhaps the most remarkable thing about these early shirts from the 1900s is the colour, more a yellow than the shade of Old Gold the club was to become famous for.

1908 was a big year for Wolves, who won their second FA Cup final, the underdogs beating Newcastle 3-1 before a crowd of 75,000 at Crystal Palace.

Mind you, red and white stripes, even blue and white hoops had been worn in the early days, so it wasn't that radical!

This shirt was worn by Billy Caddick, who played 36 of the 42 games that season. Despite only losing three times in the division, Wolves only beat second-placed Rochdale to promotion by a single point.

With the club demoted from the top two divisions for the first time, they opted for a change of strip to bring about a change in fortunes.

The stripes of the past 30 years gone, in came a yellow shirt with an unusual dark 'V' front and back, and white shorts to replace the previously standard black.

Apart from the following season when they briefly reverted back to stripes, white shorts would remain right through the 1920s.

This was the only season Wolves wore this design, more familiar on a rugby pitch or racecourse.

After the experimentation of the early '20s had continued with the introduction of two black hoops on the collar, the club finally settled on much plainer gold shirts with a black button-up collar.

This was in a darker shade which became known as 'Wolves Old Gold', and there would be few variations to this colour or design over the following quarter of a century.

The shirt pictured was worn by Charlie Phillips, who played over 200 games for the Molineux men, scoring 65 goals between 1930 and 1936.

Although shirt numbers were seen for the first time when Everton visited for the last game of the 1932/33 season, it was another six years before Wolves adopted them in their 5-0 rout of Grimsby Town in the FA Cup semi-final in 1939 (which still holds Old Trafford's record attendance, 76,962).

With numbers now a permanent fixture, the club's first honour wearing them came in 1949, winning the FA Cup for the third time with a 3-1 victory over Leicester City at Wembley.

The number seven pictured was worn by the legendary Johnny Hancocks in that game, the start of a real 'Golden Era' for Wolverhampton Wanderers Football Club.

CHARLIE PHILLIPS.
Wolverhampton Wanderers F.C.
TOPICAL TOBS.

Possibly the most historically important shirt in my collection and definitely the rarest, this fluorescent gold beauty was made famous by those epic mid-'50s nights under the floodlights against exotic opposition. Made by local seamstresses out of rayon – or 'poor man's silk' – the shirts were designed to show up well under the newly installed lights.

The idea was that Wolves would take on the world's finest teams, and they did just that, playing Racing Club of Argentina, Tel Aviv, South Africa and Spartak Moscow, to name but a few. The most famous game came against Honved, revered throughout Europe and featuring a number of Hungarian internationals from the team that had demolished England 6-3 at Wembley, led by the great Ferenc Puskás.

After coming from 2-0 behind at half-time to win 3-2, Wolves were proclaimed 'Champions of the World' by several English publications, which led to French paper *L'Equipe* reacting angrily to the British arrogance and calling for a continental trophy to decide who really was the best. As a result, the European Cup came into being, now known as the Champions League.

The shirt featured was worn by Jimmy Murray versus Moscow Dynamo, played 11 months after the Honved triumph.

In 1956, Wolves moved away from the famous Old Gold shirt they had proudly worn for more than 25 years. The black button collar was replaced by a deep 'V' neck on a much lighter shade of gold. The long sleeves of the past were also gone, the cuffs on the new shirt trimmed in black.

Having won their first League

title in 1953/54, Wolves again became Champions of England in 1957/58 and 1958/59, followed by a fourth FA Cup victory in May 1960.

The shirt pictured was worn by Barry Stobart in English football's showpiece occasion and featured the Wolverhampton coat of arms, embroidered big and bold on the left breast.

It was a fitting end to the most successful period the club had

ever seen, winning two FA Cups and three League titles while being proclaimed 'Champions of the World' by the British press.

Only a handful of clubs have shown such dominance over a decade in English football, and the 1950s were most definitely Wolverhampton Wanderers' golden years.

Possibly the blandest shirt the club have ever worn, certainly in the Umbro period, but this by one of the most charismatic players ever to grace the Old Gold and Black. In a fading team, Peter 'Knocker' Knowles burst on to the scene quite brilliantly, and by 1965/66 Wolves had a fast-emerging superstar on their hands.

One of the best young players in the land, he was being compared with the legendary George Best, coincidentally also a Wolves fan growing up. Here was a major star in the making. Flamboyant, fashionable and with the looks to match, the ladies adored him.

One young girl made a bee-line for Derek Dougan to ask for a shirt as a souvenir and, ever the gentleman, he agreed – only to be met by the response, "Peter Knowles', please!" And that's how the shirt ended up in my collection 40 years later.

Peter shocked everyone by walking away from the game to become a Jehovah's Witness in 1970. He was just 23 and had scored 61 goals in his 174 appearances, the club retaining his contract for a further 10 years.

I was lucky enough to meet Peter for a coffee five years ago and asked him if he ever regretted the decision.

"Not once," was the reply.

Until now, the only badge ever to appear on a Wolves shirt was the town's coat of arms, on Cup-final occasions. But in 1970/71, the 'WW' icon appeared with a single leaping wolf positioned above the lettering. Our first club badge.

There were two styles of shirt used, a round-necked and a collared version, both featuring black neck and cuffs. The round neck was worn when winning the inaugural Texaco Cup and again on the thrilling, goal-laden journey to the UEFA Cup final in 1971/72, but fold-down collars were in permanently the following season. Despite losing in both the FA Cup and League Cup semi-finals that campaign, more success was just around the corner.

The shirt featured was worn by Derek Dougan versus Spurs at

Molineux in August 1970. 'The Doog' generally wore the number ten shirt, only wearing number nine five times that season. Photographic evidence from back in the '70s can be in short supply, but in this instance it proved the already excellent provenance to be spot-on.

The first game at Wembley I attended with my dad, and the first Aertex shirt in the book.

First appearing in the late '60s, and then adopted by England in 1969 as a cooler alternative to the standard shirt, Wolves followed suit a couple of years later. The fashion gathered momentum over subsequent years and Wolves were in the new fabric when they proudly emerged from the Wembley tunnel for the 1974 League Cup final versus Manchester City. Despite being underdogs, the Molineux men won their first major trophy since 1960.

The shirt was a thing of beauty: three leaping Wolves centre stage, Umbro logo on the right breast

and 'Wembley 1974' on the left.

After the game, Frank Munro famously swapped his shirt on the pitch, only to give away Denis Law's to one of the ball boys! The kitman at the time kept most of the matchworn shirts, giving the players their spare unworn to keep – the reason for this only coming to light many years later.

Bizarrely, the shirt was also worn in a few League games of what remained of that season, and again a full 12 months later!

WONDERFUL WOLVES!

1974 FOOTBALL LEAGUE CUP FINAL

OFFICIAL SOUVENIR RECORD ALBUM   Match commentary highlights

Two changes to the shirt from the one worn so successfully against Manchester City. Here we see a much larger Umbro badge and 'FL Cup Winners 1974' subtly embroidered on the left breast.

It's another rarely seen shirt, this one surviving simply because it was never worn in a match, the number 14 only being used for the season's squad photo.

No shirts were ever wasted by the Molineux kit men in those days. As previously mentioned, the League Cup final shirts were worn occasionally this season. Worn shirts would then be recycled for use in training, usually with a number added on the front in felt tip; and then finally, once they started to fall apart, they would be ripped into cloths and used for cleaning the bath or players' boots.

One shirt that appeared this season did cause a few problems both for me personally and for other collectors – so much so that we couldn't work out what had happened until after the first book was published. Umbro were asked to produce a set of League Cup final shirts as keepsakes for the directors and staff at the club and, as often happens, years later some found their way on to the open market. They were almost exact copies, fully embroidered, player-specification neck label right, even down to the number on the back including the stitching.

Look at the picture below then go back and compare to the shirt the players wore. Can you spot the two obvious differences none of us initially picked up on?

DIVISION II.
CHAMPIONS
1976-77

Gone was the 'Cup Winners' embroidery of the previous season, now replaced by a new, horizontal-style 'WW'. This particular shirt had been missing from my collection until we were doing some work not long after the Covid lockdown.

A delivery driver was on the last drop of his day, and I helped him with it. Noticing my Wolves shorts, he asked if I went to the games; but before I could answer, my wife informed him that I was Wolves mad and had my own museum.

"I've got an old Umbro shirt," came the reply. "Frank Munro was my dad's mate." And less than two hours later it was hanging proudly in the collection.

Forever remembered as a relegation shirt the first season it was worn, then thankfully a promotion shirt the next, it's been stained by tears and sprayed with champagne in equal measure.

Having never been out of the top flight for a decade, the club stormed the old Second Division, outscoring all rivals by some distance on our way to lifting the title. Alan Sunderland's Division Two Champions plaque is pictured above.

382 FRANK MUNRO

Voted Wolverhampton Wanderers' best shirt of all time, it's hard to disagree with the democratic view of the fans.

Without a doubt, the Umbro shirts over a 15-year period were all superb but this one had everything. The letters 'WW' were again offset, finishing a classic look that I doubt will ever be beaten.

This was worn around the time of the 1979 FA Cup semi-final defeat, judging by the size of the collar, hardly worn and unwashed – a rarity from this period. We know it hasn't been washed because Umbro's 'The Choice of Champions' transfer is intact on the bottom of the shirt. A couple of washes and they were gone.

I'm told it was worn by Steve Daley but, back in the day, the

shirts were used in all types of games and could even have been worn a season or two later in a testimonial or a friendly.

Sadly, more and more fakes from this period are coming on to the market to satisfy demand, and they're getting harder to spot. There are at least two giveaways, no matter how 'good' the counterfeit, so always check with an expert before parting with your hard-earned money. Remember the good advice I was given many years ago: if it seems too good to be true, it most likely is!

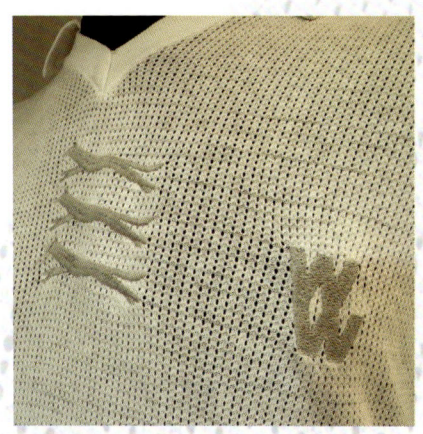

winter, the classy all-white kit the players started in didn't look the same after 90 minutes!

A normal wash was not enough to get the shirts back to pristine white so bleach was added to the normal powder. It did the job but also turned the black embroidery light grey. The black numbers were

Wolverhampton Wanderers wore a white change shirt right up to the 1990/91 season; but because our Old Gold and Black rarely clashes with opposition colours, its appearances were few and far between. Blackpool was one away fixture where it featured, due to their distinctive tangerine shirts. Norwich was another, up against canary yellow, and it's hard to recall Wolves playing at Hull or Oxford in our traditional strip.

The shirt was definitely worn in the 1978/79 FA Cup quarter-final replay versus Shrewsbury Town. Coming at the end of a severe

not affected apart from the cotton stitching which also faded.

Combine this rough treatment with the light Aertex fabric and it's no surprise so few survived. The main photo is a prepared shirt: no number, thus never worn. The photos on this page are of my matchworn shirt which clearly shows the result of bleach cleaning.

The 1979/80 season began with the players wearing the same strip as the previous – up until 17th November versus Coventry, when they ran out wearing a new shirt complete with a new club badge! Unlike today, when a shirt launch is big news, this came as a shock to everyone, not least the male streaker.

The three leaping wolves had been replaced in favour of a large, stylised wolf's head with 'Wolves' embroidered beneath.

On 15th March 1980 the players walked out at Wembley to take on Nottingham Forest with special additional embroidery around the motif. Arranged in an arc were the

thrilling words, '1979-80 Football League Cup Final Wembley'.

Despite being massive underdogs, up against Brian Clough's European champions, Wolves once again finished triumphant. The shirt pictured was worn throughout the whole game by Kenny Hibbitt, who afterwards swapped with Martin O'Neill.

Despite Martin's wife's best efforts, she never did quite get all of the massive chalk mark off the back of the shirt. The best provenance you can get!

Not often does a team wear two totally different shirts in one season, let alone on the way to qualifying for Europe twice! But Wolves effectively did just that by winning the League Cup and finishing sixth in the top division.

In the second half of the season Wolves visited Norwich twice, in the League and in a fourth-round FA Cup replay. Peter Daniel wore number four in both games, and then again the following season in the League match at Carrow Road.

This was the first shirt I ever purchased at auction, and a valuable lesson was learnt that day. Along with an Andy Mutch Mercantile Credit matchworn, it was bid up much higher than I was hoping or expecting, and eventually I had to admit defeat on the former. A couple of days later I found out that a top shirt collector, and now trusted friend, was the person bidding against me in the online auction and would happily have stood aside had he known I was the other bidder!

Many years later he sold it to me, so just maybe patience is a virtue.

Wolves' first ever shirt with a sponsor's logo also goes down as my personal all-time favourite. At the time this shocked the traditionalists, featuring not only a black pinstripe but also a 'V' neck with two black stripes sandwiching a gold one as trim.

None of the detailing represented anything new to a Wolverhampton Wanderers kit, but combined with 'Tatung' boldly emblazoned across the shirt, many thought it went several steps too far.

However, the club were in a bad way financially, having faced the real threat of extinction just a few

weeks earlier, and the additional revenue from the new source of sponsorship was welcomed with open arms.

Kenny Hibbitt was in the twilight of his career by now but still did his sweat-soaked shirt proud. He was one of the very best to ever grace the Molineux turf.

For 16 years he gave everything for the Old Gold and Black, making over 570 appearances and scoring 114 goals, including one in the 1974 League Cup final.

the mid '80s, even the local papers didn't send a photographer to many of them!

The shirt featured here was used away at Shrewsbury Town in December 1982, when Wayne Clarke scored both goals in a 2-0 win. His partnership with Andy Gray helped Wolves back to the top division; but the euphoria was short lived.

When the Tatung sponsorship came along, Umbro had been the kit brand of choice at Molineux for well over two decades; despite 1982-86 being remembered for the club dropping from the First to Fourth Division in successive seasons, the style and quality of the shirts remained unmatched.

Although I went to every game in that period, there were two change shirts that I couldn't remember until my collecting became serious – and this is the first.

Programmes are a fantastic source for researching when and how often a particular shirt was worn, but it was the *Express & Star* archives that came up trumps in my search for a photo of Wolves wearing this one.

We take it for granted today, a high-definition record of every match; but it got that bad during

The most frequent question I'm asked by visitors viewing the collection is, "Which shirt is your favourite?" For a home shirt, there are several, but the away shirt is easy.

If it's possible to fall in love with a football shirt at first sight, then I must plead guilty.

This was the final offering from Umbro and, in my humble opinion, they saved the best until last. In many ways, it shouldn't work, sequential silver and white bold stripes highlighted by black pinstripes, with thin blue pinstripes between the gold and black on both collar and cuffs.

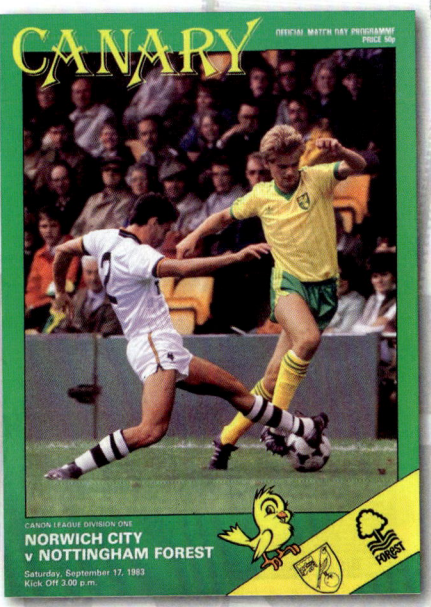

When you look back at the previous away offerings, Umbro only ever used two colours, white with black trimmings, so this was a radical way to bring the curtain down on what had been a dream partnership.

There's a saying that 'beauty is in the eye of the beholder', and that perfectly sums up most people's reaction to this shirt.

Matchworn, muddy and unwashed by Mel Eves. Perfection.

For many Wolves shirt collectors this is considered the holy grail. Only one example sporting the Benjamin Perry sponsor is known to have survived, and it's displayed in the superb Molineux museum.

For much of the season, Wolves wore the shirt featured opposite, but without a sponsor logo after Tatung ended their backing. With the club on a seemingly unstoppable downward spiral, both on and off the field, it seemed it would stay that way until Walsall builders' merchants Benjamin Perry became only the second sponsor to appear on the Old Gold and Black.

A simple cloth patch was quickly printed and on 8th March 1986 the shirt made its debut along

with young Andy Mutch. One prospered and earned a place in Wolverhampton Wanderers' Hall of Fame, the other came and went rather more quickly.

When the season ended in another relegation the sponsor patches were removed, the shirts used for training in preparation for life in the Fourth Division.

At this point the club needed a miracle. No one could have foreseen it would arrive in the form of a Tipton skinhead signed from West Bromwich Albion.

Talking to many former players from the 1970s and '80s, it became apparent that, unlike today, the kitmen of the time did not like letting players have their shirts under any circumstances. Members of the '74 and '80 League Cup-winning teams were mostly given their spare unworn shirt, the kitman keeping the other. Back then, the players were issued with two shirts, one long-sleeved, the other short, so it isn't difficult to work out the matchworn ones.

There were exceptions, of course. Andy Gray kept his; Ken Hibbitt and Geoff Palmer swapped with Forest players, for example; but most players received their match issued. This left a fair amount of matchworn shirts unaccounted for from both finals, kit now worth thousands of pounds each. Why haven't any of them come on to the open market, especially during Covid when prices went sky high?

During research for the first book, two people came forward and told the exact same story, even though neither knew the other. In the early 1990s, during the renovation of the Waterloo Road Stand – now the Billy Wright – they were walking past Molineux and noticed something strange in a skip. There were cardboard boxes covered in rubble... and sticking out of one was what looked like strips of material. Upon closer inspection, the Umbro arm detailing could be seen, at which point both men pulled out a 1977-79 matchworn shirt and made a hasty exit. But why would a box containing historic and obviously desirable shirts ever be thrown on a skip?

A few years later, before the second book was published, I was in conversation with a guy who turned out to be one of the builders on the project, and I told him the story. Without hesitation he replied that yes, the boxes were from 'the locked room'. They were demolishing an area

of the Waterloo Road Stand that contained a room to which they could find no key; they were told to get on with the job and smash it down. The room turned out to be full of boxes packed with shirts from various seasons. The boss on the project made a call to inform the club, but the reply was clear: "That area's got to be cleared today. Put the boxes on the skip."

In those days, skips went straight to landfill, so we must now believe that hundreds of shirts dating from 1970 up to the end of the Umbro era were deliberately destroyed.

There's plenty of evidence that old shirts were used in training, worn kit having been set aside in previous eras as part of a frugal, long-term recycling regime. Graham Hawkins managed Wolves from 1982-84, and this training photo clearly shows players in various seasons' shirts, the rarest being the round-necked away 1970-72 being worn by Andy Gray.

Only now are we able to guess where the kitman stored all the old shirts, only removing a few when needed for training or testimonial games.

Wolves started the season languishing in the Fourth Division, with no sponsor and wearing last season's shirt minus the Benjamin Perry sponsor panel. Things took an unexpected turn in October when Staw Distribution took out a page in the programme for the Orient match announcing a new sponsorship deal and shirt.

The new kit got off to the worst possible start, being worn in the infamous FA Cup defeat to non-league Chorley. Watching in the stands were Wolves' two new signings from West Bromwich Albion, Steve Bull and Andy Thompson, who had arrived for a combined fee of £65,000 but were ineligible for the first-round tie.

'Bully' made his debut on 22nd November 1986 versus Wrexham, with his first goal coming just ten days later in an Associate Members Cup game away to Cardiff. Another 305 goals were to follow, and in 13 years with Wolves Bull broke four of the club's goalscoring records, including 18 hat-tricks.

This shirt originally came from his manager/agent who secured it after Bully started scoring and his popularity quickly began to grow. Because it was the same number nine he had worn in every game,

he thought its value would lie in it being his debut shirt, not realising that he wore the number eight in that game. This was also the season that Bull wore a long-sleeved shirt, the one and only time during his Wolves career.

Bull went on to score 19 goals in his first season, Wolves finishing fourth but losing out to Aldershot in the Play-offs. He would go on to wear the number nine continuously until early 1993/94, when he wore the number 14 shirt for an Anglo-Italian Cup game at home to Stoke – and, true to form, climbed off the bench to score.

It's not difficult to find shirts or inspiration for these two seasons. Here we had arguably the greatest signing Wolves ever made, the resurgence of a fallen giant and no less than three variations of the home shirt, two worn at Wembley!

Stephen George Bull, from Tipton to Turin – a story so outlandish it reads more like a fairy tale than an international footballer's biography. The most prolific number nine in the club's entire history made his Wolves debut in the Staw shirt, but not in the number he is most famous for. That honour went to Andy Mutch, with Bully turning out in the number eight instead.

There's much more of Bull to follow but those first two seasons were as much about Andy Mutch and Robbie Dennison, another two legends who played a huge part in awakening the sleeping giant.

The standard shirt featured additional embroidery for the first visit to the Twin Towers, 'Football League Centenary Finalists 1988' proudly wrapped around the badge for the 16-club weekend tournament held in mid April. Wolves went out in our first game against Everton, on penalties, the event best remembered for Robbie Dennison's 25-yard rocket that left Neville Southall sprawling in the back of the net.

The goal was so good that Sky's Johnny Phillips did a piece on it for *Soccer Saturday* many years later, titled 'The Best Wembley Goal You've Never Seen.'

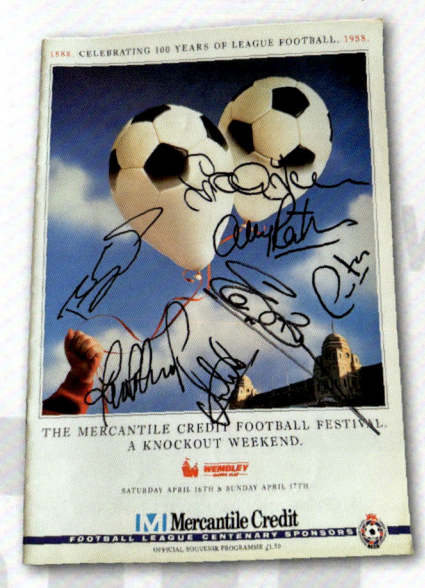

Just a few weeks after his stunning Wembley goal in the Centenary Final tournament, Robbie Dennison took centre stage again.

Another subtle alteration to the crest saw 'Wembley 88' added in an arc above the wolf's head. Money was still very tight at Molineux so each player had just one shirt each. 45,000-plus Wolves fans were in the 80,841 crowd to watch the Fourth Division showpiece with Burnley. Andy Mutch put the Molineux men 1-0 up before Robbie dispatched a trademark free-kick round the wall into the top corner of the net.

Wolves were once more on the rise. Bully obviously received most of the praise but this was a proper team, brilliantly put together by manager Graham Turner.

This was also the year that Wolves shirt sales really took off. Original replicas of the two Wembley finals shirts in mint condition now fetch hundreds of pounds, the white versions even more.

The giant was awake, money was pouring into the club shop and the players had a new highlight of the week, training on the concrete car park behind the North Bank with traffic cones for goals – having first 'bounced' any cars out of the way.

Those really were the days...

As champions of Division Four in 1987/88, Wolves became the first team to have won all four divisions of the Football League. The juggernaut was moving forward nicely, Steve Bull's 52 goals in all competitions a new club record.

A new sponsor, Manders Paint & Ink, had their logo on display across a smart new shirt made by Scoreline. 1988/89 saw the manufacturer's logo displayed on each arm, but visibility issues saw a larger version moved to the right breast the following season. The embroidered crest and machine-stitched numbers were the major differences from the replica, now being sold in large quantities.

A 'Steve Bull Special' match shirt was produced by Scoreline, a limited edition of 750 made to commemorate Bully's record-breaking scoring feats. Featuring a sewn-on number nine, an embroidered club crest and biro signature in the centre, these are sometimes passed off as matchworn, but signature placement and a printed Scoreline logo are the giveaways.

That man Bull? On 29th January 1989 he took his goal tally to over 100 after just two years at the club, scoring a hat-trick in the 3-0 victory over Bristol City. A second successive promotion as Third Division champions followed, his 50 goals taking him to a record 102 in just two quite incredible seasons.

August 1990: Bully back from the World Cup in Italy, Wolves in the Second Division, and Sir Jack safely installed as the new owner of his beloved Wolverhampton Wanderers.

With Goodyear taking over as main sponsors, there was a feel-good factor around Molineux, and a stunning new Scoreline kit to match. For the first time, Football League emblems were stitched on to each arm, the club crest again embroidered into the shirt.

Scoreline were already in financial trouble before a global fabric shortage kicked in and sadly triggered Wolves' commercial team's decision to cut links with the manufacturer. Replica sales

had taken off, and the club feared an inability to satisfy demand.

Bukta came in at short notice, replacing Scoreline's shadow-printed chessboard effect with a wolves' head pattern. Unsurprisingly, having only been used in a handful of fixtures, the matchworn Scoreline are now highly prized by collectors, the away shirt even rarer than the home.

The 1991/92 season ended with 32 booby-trap devices buried in the pitch before the final game with Middlesbrough, followed by an arson attack at the ground. Surely the next shirt would be relatively drama free...

After all the problems with the previous season's shirt, you might have thought the club would go with a safe option, especially producing it under their own brandname, 'Molineux'.

The design that launched the new label was radical, to say the least, and was at the time the most unpopular Wolves shirt ever made. Known as the 'Tyre Track', an unsuccessful campaign was launched by supporters to get it changed, but it wasn't only the fans who shared this opinion.

After the first book came out, I was approached by one of the main guys behind the production of the shirt, who told me the real story. They already had two excellent shirts to present to the club for approval but had been asked to offer three. Struggling for a third, they noticed a plain roll used for the other designs but with pieces of discarded black fabric scattered around. Straight away, they decided to go with this pattern in the style of the other two shirts.

Billy Wright was present at the all-important meeting along with a guest from Telford. The three shirts were placed on the table, the designers confident the final shirt would be quickly eliminated. But, to their dismay, Billy asked the visitor from Telford what he thought – and the rest is history.

The shirt was so unpopular it only lasted one season, but is now considered a relatively rare classic by collectors. Also, because the pattern was totally random, no two shirts are the same.

The Molineux brand's first attempt at an away shirt fared slightly better than the home, and did at least last for the expected two seasons.

It's another that wasn't popular at the time but is now considered a cult classic, infamously remembered for its pairing with red shorts in an early appearance versus Oxford in August 1992. There are various rumours regarding why Wolves wore Oxford shorts that day but the most likely explanation is that the kitman did indeed forget to pack the shorts!

With a design arguably well ahead of its time, these shirts

were also well made with quality materials that have stood the test of time much better than many of the modern, mass-produced kits.

The following season, our trip to Oxford again sparked plenty of discussions, but this time it wasn't the kit everyone was talking about. Graham Turner was gone, judged to have fallen short at the final hurdle, with Graham Taylor installed as his replacement.

Could the former England manager be the man to finally return the club to the top division?

The third and final offering under the Molineux brand, and they definitely saved the best 'til last. Some of the sacred elements of a Wolverhampton Wanderers kit had at last been restored, giving a more traditional feel. A black buttoned collar and cuffs combined with a 1970s shade of Old Gold could never fail, especially with an embroidered town crest and manufacturer's logo further complementing what is plainly a great shirt.

Although Sir Jack had loosened the purse strings for transfers, the kitman was still working to the same budget, with players only allowed two or three shirts per season. Our big marquee signing, however, was an early exception, Geoff Thomas famously having the 'D' ripped off the 'Goodyear' logo in a September Black Country derby at the Hawthorns.

The shirt featured may well also have been worn in that game, both Bull and Thomas scoring in the 2-3 defeat. It is one of many I own that were originally part of the John 'Foz' Hendley collection. A legend at Wolves, he was a fan for over 50 years, with almost 20 of them spent working at his beloved Molineux. From matchday programme editor to club historian and author of several excellent books, 'Foz' is sadly missed by all who knew him, and I would like to dedicate this page in his memory.

The question I'm asked most often about matchworn collecting is, "Where do you get them from?" There are several different sources, and this shirt is a good example of one obtained direct from a player's own collection.

When I started in 2009 there wasn't much of a Wolves collecting community at all, and shirts could be picked up cheaply in comparison to today's prices. An example I often use is an Umbro '70s shirt which sold for £300, and would now command ten times more – if only you could find one. That was from eBay, still a source I would recommend, but only if you know what you're doing.

Don't be afraid to ask the sellers questions, and always do your research. Even the very best have been stung.

Obtaining a shirt direct from a player provides the best provenance you can possibly get. During the 1994/95 season the number 11 was largely worn by Robbie and Steve Froggatt, so it wouldn't otherwise have been possible to say for sure who had worn it.

American-owned Nutmeg took over kit production with a shirt almost identical to the last one, apart from the manufacturer's logo and larger Football League arm patches.

A John De Wolf hat-trick at Port Vale will always stick in the memory from this season, and I was excited to visit the man who had his unwashed shirt off his back. Sadly, he gave it to a young lad to play football in and neither were ever seen again, a story I've heard far too many times.

After the brief flirtation with blue, it was back to the traditional change kit of over 100 years. The Nutmeg shirt was a white version of the home, and a stunning one at that. It even got an airing in Europe, in the revised Anglo-Italian Cup, when Wolves visited Lecce.

Worn by Neil Emblen during 1994/95, the season ended in heartbreak for Wolves, losing the Play-off semi-final to Bolton. Who can ever forget the image of Bully slumped in despair after the final whistle?

This was also the season the club lost its most famous son, Billy Wright CBE, captain of club and country through the 1950s when Wolves were champions of England

in 1954, 1958 and 1959, and lifted the FA Cup in 1949.

He was the first player in the world to reach 100 caps for his country and was never once cautioned throughout his entire career. He was also ever present in the mid-1950s floodlit friendlies, the catalyst to European cup competition.

His statue now proudly on display outside the main stand named in his honour, Billy Wright epitomised everything Wolverhampton Wanderers stood for throughout the golden period in the club's history.

1953-54   1957-58   1958-59

An excellent effort once again from Nutmeg, and a first in that the shirt available to the fans was actually the same as that worn by the players, making it a good option for the fakers.

The good news is that although the Football League patches are readily available, the numbers aren't. I saw a couple last year which were very close to the match issue but they had mistakenly added the player's name above the number, which didn't really begin until 1999.

The shirt shown was worn by Don Goodman, and features the official felt number used for 1995/96. I also own another example with the previous season's machine-stitched number. It came from John Hendley's collection, a

number 12 in mint condition. At first, I couldn't understand why it had the 'wrong' numbers on it, until I discovered that the new shirt was first worn in the final two games of the previous season, the Play-off semi-finals against Bolton Wanderers. The number 12 in both legs was Brian Laws, remembered more for his bus-driving antics than his football during his time at the club.

The 'V'-neck shirt features subtle, high-quality 'W.W.F.C.' embroidery around the crest, and 'Wolves' and the coat of arms are imprinted into the fabric. It all adds up to a very classy look for a shirt now in high demand amongst collectors.

'll start with a confession on this one: I don't like it; but I do recognise that I'm in a tiny minority. Steve Bull summed it up well: it's not just the design, it's how baggy and ungainly it is, which "made it easy for the defenders to grab hold of you."

In order to fit the fashion of the times (rather than the player), they were all made at least one size too big, possibly two. Matchworn by Robbie Keane, this shirt is a prime example. For the first few months white numbers were used but it quickly became apparent that when washed they turned grey, forcing the change to black.

It's certainly a design recognised instantly as Wolves, and the keeper shirts especially are now considered classics. For the purist, there was simply too much black.

I always love a shirt with a story, and this is one of my favourites.

Both Steve Bull and Robbie Keane had both surprisingly been left out of the starting line-up for the FA Cup semi-final with Arsenal. Sitting on the bench until very late in the game, Wolves losing 1-0, they were both sent on but too late to make any difference. Robbie was called to do a TV interview at the final whistle, and when it concluded he presented a young Villa Park ball boy with his shirt... which he then sold on eBay 15 years later, unwashed and with photographic proof.

A beautiful August afternoon heralded the start to a new season and a first outing for the teal change shirt at Blundell Park. Steve Bull had been level on 16 hat-tricks with the late Billy Harthill since his last one at Derby in November 1993.

Amongst all the records Bull holds for the club, his 18 hat-tricks is a big favourite, and one that will surely never be beaten. His three goals at Grimsby took him clear outright, and the last of his hat-tricks came two years later in August 1988, in a 5-0 hammering of Barnet in a League Cup tie at Molineux in his final season with Wolves.

The shirt was the same design as the home, but worked much better in the green/blue teal colourway. When we asked Kirsty Bull which picture was Steve's favourite, so we could get it painted as a surprise for his *They Wore the Shirt* tribute dinner, her answer

was instant: "Grimsby aeroplane celebration, he loves that."

Bully always gave his shirts away, often to charities, which is how this was obtained. A few weeks after the game he took it along to a fundraiser at a working men's club, where it went to the lucky winner of a grand prize raffle.

For the second successive year Wolves took to the field on day one of the season sporting a new away shirt, and the fans once again had some individual heroics to savour along with another three away points.

Although Bully wore this shirt in the game, it was a young lad only weeks past his 17th birthday who took the plaudits at Carrow Road. Two special strikes from Robbie Keane disposed of Norwich, ensuring that when most fans see the white and teal kit, the first player they think of is the dazzling Irish youth international.

It's another highly underrated design elevated by the wolf's head on the collar and those printed into the white fabric.

This was only added to my collection recently and again shows the unlikely places shirts can be found. A good friend of Bully asked him to open a new pub at the end of the season, and he took his shirt along as a gift. They weren't the value they are today, and the goalscoring legend regularly gave them away throughout his career and beyond. Just one example of his generosity was the World Cup Italia 1990 matchworn England shirt that Bully gifted to Colin Lee after his retirement in 1999.

I'm often asked how I store my shirts, and in my opinion the best option is to seal them in a clear plastic bag, after being air dried, with the game details on a label stuck on the outside. These can then be kept in strong plastic boxes designed to slide under beds.

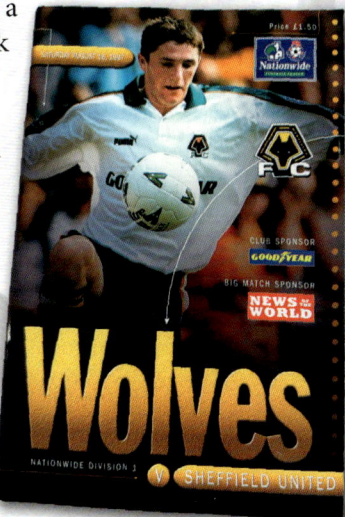

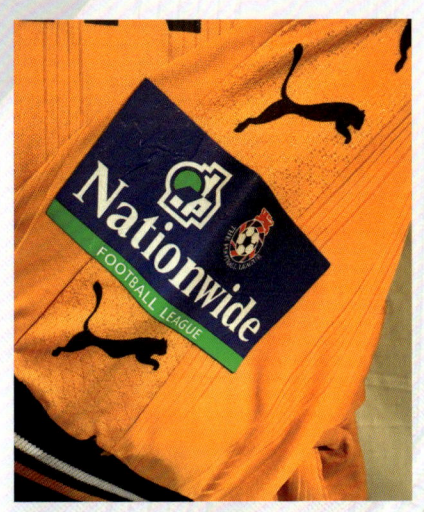

The second tier of English football finally fell into line with the Premier League in 1999 by agreeing to feature player's names above their shirt numbers.

This should have been music to the ears of matchworn collectors, but for me it was totally overshadowed by the preseason news that Steve Bull was having to retire due to injury. My favourite player, and the man who had given me memories I will take to the grave, would never again wear the Old Gold and Black with 'Bull' emblazoned above the famous number nine.

I had recently carried my beloved Gran's coffin into church without showing any emotion, but when Bully walked out on to the Molineux turf to take the acclaim

of the fans one final time I was in bits, and everyone reading this lucky enough to have witnessed those years will know exactly what I mean.

Due to that association, I have no affection for this shirt, which is unfair because it was another great design by Puma: a nice shade of gold with a smart trim and collar. Feedback from the original book told me people looked first for their favourite shirt and second the one they disliked the most. If there were a third option of a shirt you really should like but don't, this would win hands down.

The away shirt that marked the switch over from 20th century to 21st was the same colour that had served the club so well from 1907 through to 1990.

We use the term 'away' but given the the amount of times Wolves wear the home kit when playing away, it should really be called the 'change' shirt.

I picked this one to highlight another point that collectors can often miss, and that is awareness of players' available and preferred sleeve options.

Like Paul Ince, Kenny Miller and many others, Steve Sedgley preferred to wear a long-sleeved shirt even on the warmest of days. There are always exceptions to such rules, but a little research and insider knowledge can provide a good starting point when checking matchworn provenance.

A classic example of this was Nathan Blake and the riddle of his shirt in the 2003 Play-off final, which confounded me for years.

I was lucky enough to own both his long- and short-sleeved shirts at one time, and each of them them had allegedly been worn during the big match; however, the match video showed that he wore short-sleeved all game.

A short conversation with Nathan quickly solved the mystery: he'd come out for the warm-up in his long-sleeved but it was so hot inside the Millennium Stadium that back in the dressing room the kitman taped them up on the inside for the first half; then he changed into his short-sleeved in the second half.

Referring back to the video, it's clear that first-half short sleeves are indeed slightly longer!

his head, at which point Michael Branch came running over, fearing he was being attacked! Muscat quickly explained and Greg, not one to miss an opportunity, told Branch, "I'll have yours as well!"

On the train home he unveiled his prized souvenirs, which caught the eye of a young woman who must have been one of Muscat's biggest fans. Let's just say she gave Greg a very persuasive look. He submitted to her demands in gentlemanly fashion, and off she went with a Michael Branch shirt!

Wolves turned the clocks back as they entered the first full season of the new Millennium. A distinctly new look for the younger supporters, rustlike in colour that was last used in the glory days of 1930-54 – Wolves Old Gold.

The truth is that it wasn't very popular, especially when wet under the floodlights, 'drab' being a fair description.

This shirt was given to me by master carpenter and good friend Greg Elliott, last worn by Kevin Muscat in the 2-0 victory at Crystal Palace, 20th April 2001. At the final whistle Greg jumped on to the pitch and asked Muscat for his shirt who gladly obliged. Being soaking wet, he helped him pull it over

Nothing sets off a Wolves shirt better than quality embroidery, especially when it includes the word 'final'.

We'd previously had the 1974 and 1980 League Cup finals, and now this, arguably every bit as important. The 2002/03 First Division Play-off final had Premier League riches awaiting the winner. On the day everything just clicked, and Sheffield United were simply blown away at the Millennium Stadium in Cardiff.

Initially the Admiral shirt got a battering from critics and fans alike, mainly because of the sponsor, but quickly grew in popularity the nearer we got to the final. Recent years have seen

several replica shirts embroidered and badged up like the matchworn, something that caused much debate amongst the top collectors. I personally have no doubt whatsoever that some of these will be sold as matchworn in years to come, the Doritos shirts already being the most commonly faked of that era. Paul Ince was a great player for Wolves but the number of his shirts I've seen for sale is laughable and alarming in equal measure. Again, I can't stress the point too strongly, provenance and proof of origin is more important than ever with this shirt.

This is another of those 'did he, didn't he?' shirts. I certainly can't remember Lescott wearing this shirt in short-sleeved, hence it's listed as 'match prepared'.

What do you do if you've been told a shirt is matchworn but have your doubts? It's a lot more difficult with the older shirts but easier nowadays. With this shirt, for example, a quick Google search of 'Wolves 2002/03' brings up several videos, *Wolverhampton Wanderers FC Review of the Season* being the best by far. This takes you through the complete season, game by game, and is invaluable to shirt collectors. Pre internet, in the '90s, it was all done in book form – if you haven't got these publications,

you should consider them, as they only cost a few pounds for each season and are generally readily available on eBay.

With high-definition photos online, it's so easy now, especially in Premier League games. Photo matching can be done even with a clean shirt, because the name, numbers and patches are all put on by hand. There's one particular season where you can even tell who printed the shirt up! Kit man mistakes are not very common but, as you'll see later in the book, Wolves have had a few corkers over the years.

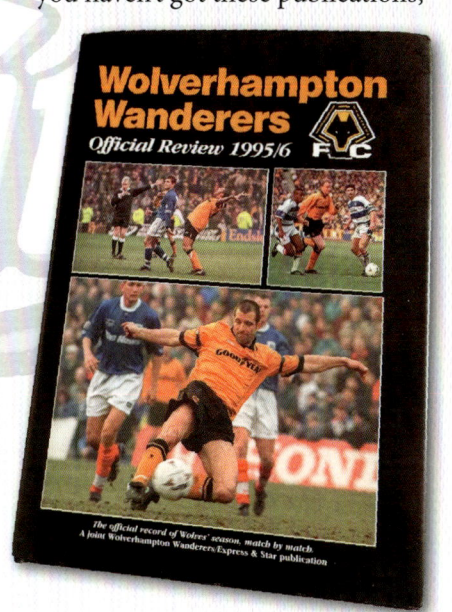

With Wolves locked into a two-year deal with Doritos, changes to the kit were always going to be minimal for the start of 2003/04.

The one subtle difference was the most important to both collectors and fans alike. Victory at the Millennium Stadium put Wolves in the Premier League for the first time and ended a 19-year absence from the top division, also ensuring a much-preferred logo featured on each arm.

This shirt was worn by Denis Irwin in his last ever professional game of football versus Spurs at Molineux on 15th May 2004. Paul Butler, understanding the significance of the shirt, had it off the kitman for his own personal

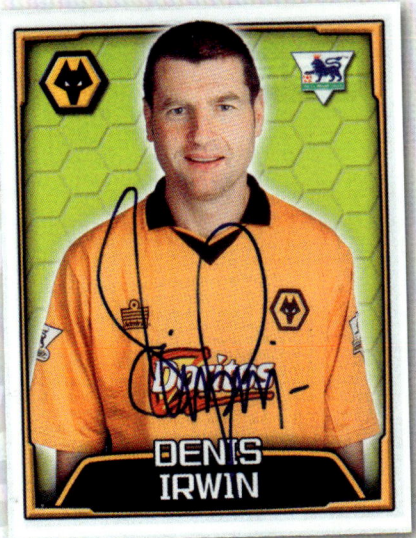

collection. 'Butts' kept everything throughout his career, including all the flags and hats thrown to the players on their victory lap in Cardiff a year earlier.

He's become a good and trusted friend, and through his charitable foundation I've been lucky enough to purchase many excellent shirts from the 2000-04 period.

This is my favourite way of obtaining matchworn kit, the provenance is second to none and you're also helping others. Everyone's a winner.

This was the first all-black kit to be used by the club and, given how the season went, it was a pretty apt choice!

I touched on the fake matchworn shirts earlier but this was the first replica Wolves shirt to be faked in big numbers. For some reason, Admiral couldn't keep up with demand in our first season in the Premier League, and an acquaintance of mine who was living in Thailand had a few shirts made locally for his mates back home in Wordsley. These were so good, other people ordered them and throughout the season hundreds were sent over, if not thousands.

When I mentioned this to an administrator on the excellent

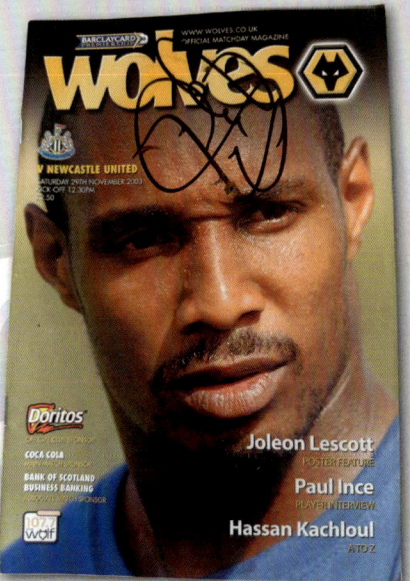

Facebook group 'Wolves FC Shirts – Buy/Sell/Show,' he was shocked, never having suspected a thing. They now spot the fakes online, and tip off members. I highly recommend joining specialist groups, this being the best for Wolves kit matchworn and replica alike. The tell-tale differences in the fakes included the club badge, neck label and Doritos sponsor. It's always worth checking authenticity before purchasing one of these, rather than leaving it until later...

Wolves' brief flirtation with the Premier League brought many changes the following season: a new sponsor in Chaucer Consulting; a new kit supplier, Le Coq Sportif; a new manager, Glenn Hoddle and, sadly, the return of Football League arm patches. The one constant was Paul Ince, still giving 100 per cent every time he wore the shirt.

The shirt had a two-year lifespan and, at first glance, both seasons were very similar... except for three differences. In 2004/05 the League patches were plastic, the numbers black and silver, and there was no sponsor on the back. For 2005/06 a reverse sponsor was added for the very first time, numbers were black with gold trim, and the arm patches changed to felt.

Both shirts pictured are muddy unwashed, the 2006 having been worn versus Plymouth Argyle on

1st April and swopped with David Norris after the game. The simple handwritten letter here is all the provenance needed.

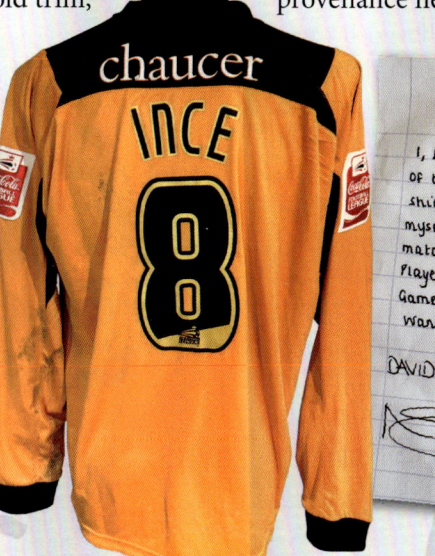

I, David Norris, confirm the authenticity of the matchworn Paul Ince home shirt. Having played in the game myself I obtained the shirt post match when swapping shirts with players.
Game: Plymouth Argyle V Wolverhampton Wanderers April 1st 2006
DAVID NORRIS

For me, this shirt always signifies the sudden departure of Glenn Hoddle and the arrival of Mick McCarthy, which is one of the reasons I like it so much.

I was so disillusioned with the style of football the previous season that I threw my season ticket away in a pub beer garden – but someone returned it!

The shirt itself was a good colour with minimal black detailing and I liked how sponsor Chaucer always tried to blend in with subtle colour changes where needed, the embroidered Le Coq Sportif logo also a bonus.

Kightly was an excellent signing from non-league Grays Athletic but was never watched by McCarthy; a club scout raved about him and the fact he could be purchased for £25,000. That was good enough for the boss, and he was quickly signed, initially on a loan deal.

This shirt was said to have been worn on his Wolves debut, something you often hear when negotiating to

buy a matchworn shirt, along with games the player scored in. This adds a bit more value but isn't always necessarily correct: I know one player who sold his own shirt and signed it 'My last goal for Wolves', genuinely believing it to be true; but it was the previous season's shirt.

The shirts I purchased were superb and covered every season he had played for Wolves.

The fact that I never kept a note of where I'd bought all the shirts I collected was a big mistake on my part. I was so wrapped up with buying everything and anything, I just didn't think about it. With hindsight, I should have kept a record of where I purchased each one, how much I paid, and the same with the ones I sold. There are now at least two shirts that I would love to buy back, but can't remember who bought them.

You can probably already guess my thoughts on this one based on the home shirt alone. One of my modern-day favourite aways, and it's white!

This is one of two I have in the collection, matchworn and unwashed by Andy Keogh: short- and long-sleeved away from 2006/07. They came from his own personal collection, but there's a twist to the story. A Leeds United collector had seen a Keogh matchworn for sale on eBay and enquired with the seller if there were any more. The answer was yes, lots of them.

He arranged to buy all the Leeds shirts, also purchasing around a dozen Wolves shirts, from memory, but possibly more. The vendor was a former partner who hadn't seen Andy for years and wanted them gone.

Afull 20 years had elapsed between winning the old Third Division under Graham Turner and the Mick McCarthy-inspired lifting of silverware in the second tier.

Wolves won it in style and with games to spare, this shirt being worn versus QPR at Molineux when Ebanks-Blake scored the goal that clinched promotion back to the Premier League – one of 25 he scored that season.

The shirt itself was another no-nonsense effort from the French manufacturer, the only noticeable difference being their logo, larger with no specific Le Coq wording and a transfer replacing the embroidered cockerel. A popular kit which goes hand in hand with an excellent season.

Another piece of advice I give people is to buy the most

popular players' shirt that you can. Defenders are generally less sought-after than forwards, for example in this current season (2023/24) a Semedo or Dawson shirt is much cheaper than Neto or Cunha. In the future it will be these stars that fans are searching for, so the shirts will hold their value better.

Dougan, Richards, Hibbitt, Bull and Mutch will always be more desirable to a collector than Parkin, Palmer, Thompson or Venus, despite them all having been superb footballers for Wolves.

The very first shirt I purchased and, in many ways, the most important. It was the catalyst for helping Dad live three years longer than predicted, for four books and most importantly £250,000 raised for various charities in his memory.

Few people know that I used to drive Bully's mum and dad down to Wembley for the England games, where we occasionally met the team coach to pick up their tickets. A couple of times I was introduced to Bobby Robson, Gazza and others, but at that time had no interest in shirts or memorabilia. At the turn of the millennium I sponsored Håvard Flo one season and Andy Sinton the next, part of the deal being you received a matchworn shirt; but both were sold on eBay.

I still don't know to this day what made me buy it other than sheer desperation, but without a doubt it's the best £50 I've ever spent. Wolves' first Premier League shirt after five years in the Championship, and the first to feature a poppy for Remembrance Day.

Like Mick McCarthy, the shirt was a no-frills effort but with much to admire, and more than did the job.

I've previously stated that a white kit with a Wolves badge on it just couldn't fail; but this one did. In fairness, it wasn't so much the shirt that was problematic as the colour of the crest.

Steve Morgan, chairman at the time, is a big Liverpool fan, and it was rumoured that his influence was behind the red detailing that included the badge. Nowadays, it's common to blend the colour of the crest to match the shirt, but go back 14 years and it was a massive own-goal.

Morgan came in for a lot of criticism during his tenure, but he was nothing short of brilliant with me – although I never did meet him in person. When I approached the club about doing the book I was met with a wall of silence and was on the verge of giving up

when a good friend sent me Steve Morgan's home address. I wrote, never expecting a reply, and was amazed when I received a letter on his own personal headed paper.

It basically gave me full access to all the shirts in the museum, with instructions to staff to give me any help I needed. Without that letter and the superb aid given by Pat Quirke and his museum staff, *They Wore the Shirt* would have been nothing more than a pipe dream. We sadly lost Pat in 2022, and I dedicate this page in his memory.

high-quality embroidery was dropped in favour of a cheaper transfer in 2014 they haven't really been the same.

When I first started collecting seriously, I wanted a matchworn version of home, away, poppy, League Cup, FA Cup, Foundation sponsor and any other specials that cropped up throughout the season, which led to me owning 500 shirts at one point.

I eventually learnt that quality beats quantity hands down, but it took me 15 years!

For the first time in seven seasons, Wolves had a new supplier's name on their match kit: Burrda Sport was formed in Switzerland as recently as 2006.

The shirt itself was a decent design, nothing groundbreaking but with the right amount of black, and back to a smart collar. The Sportingbet sponsor was never a good look, the blue and red logo doing nothing for the gold shirt; the red poppy, however, was a different story.

Worn for the first time the previous season, the embroidery was a stunning and welcome addition, this shirt being worn against Bolton Wanderers by Steven Fletcher.

I've collected the annual poppy shirts religiously but since the

Despite being the away shirt for two seasons, it was very rarely worn, with Blackpool and Norwich presenting the obvious opportunities and Manchester City and Arsenal added to the list for commercial reasons.

My favourite of all the Burrda kits, the black alternative strip really looked the part with the minimal amount of gold detailing. This shirt was worn by Kevin Doyle versus Manchester City on 29th October 2011, a game shown live on Sky Sports.

I'll hold my hands up, I never noticed the kitman's mistake during the game and, surprisingly, neither did Roger Johnson. The first he knew about it was when a mate who had watched the game on TV phoned him after the match. The kitman had put the 'N' in front of the 'H' on the back of his shirt. I tried hard to get one of the error shirts for my collection, but to no avail.

Matt Jarvis was the player that started the trend of wearing two shirts per game at Wolves in 2009/10, a practice now second nature to many Premier League players.

Forever remembered as the season it all went wrong, I could have used several players' shirts here but chose the central character, captain Roger Johnson.

The season was already going badly wrong. Mick McCarthy was sacked after a 5-1 home defeat to West Bromwich Albion, a knee-jerk decision that ultimately consigned Wolves to relegation. Terry Connor was the new manager, a position he never wanted, and then player power took over.

Things had already boiled over in

training, something I personally witnessed several times, but not on the pitch until Roger Johnson and Wayne Hennessey came head to head at home to Bolton in March. This is his unwashed shirt from that game.

I believe a club's history should be preserved, both the good and the bad, so have no problem including this infamous shirt in my collection.

This was the first season for a while that the player shirt varied from the replica, the former being 'slim fit', the latter a little more forgiving.

Wolves' 114th season of competitive league football was easily one of the worst. Richard Stearman supported a charity event after the second edition of *They Wore the Shirt* had been published and his first words were, "Thanks for using my shirt for that season!" Out of respect, I've used Sako's this time, sorry Rich.

Ståle Solbakken signed Sako, but it wasn't enough to save him from being sacked in early January after defeat to Luton in the FA Cup, the first exit to a non-league club since Chorley in 1986. Dean Saunders became the fourth permanent manager in 12 months and yet again the season ended in relegation. Going from McCarthy to Saunders in a year perfectly illustrates how bad things were; throw in Jamie O'Hara and I doubt Alex Ferguson could have kept us up!

The shirt itself didn't deserve the football that was played in it, the broad gold stripes reminiscent of Staw 1986-88, but with a smart matching collar – if only we'd had that team wearing it, managed by Graham Turner. Sadly, as noted earlier, a shirt is often judged on the season it was worn, so this one will never win any popularity votes.

Stability was needed after two successive relegations and Wolves found it in new manager Kenny Jackett. The work he did, assisted by Joe Gallen, should never be underestimated, removing the dead wood and bedding in the new players with a minimum of fuss. He's also one of the nicest managers I have ever had the pleasure of meeting.

Leigh Griffiths had been on loan at Hibs averaging a goal every couple of games until he was brought back into the fold, scoring the first goal of Kenny Jackett's Wolves reign versus Gillingham. He joined Celtic for the second

half of the season after scoring 12 goals in 26 appearances. This shirt was worn at Colchester in October, Griffiths scoring twice in a 3-0 win. Work had started on the first book by then, and Matt Murray obtained the shirt for me as a favour which I was happy to repay recently.

Fondly remembered due to the record-breaking season it was worn, I personally disliked the neck design, but it was good to see the return of both Puma and Championship football.

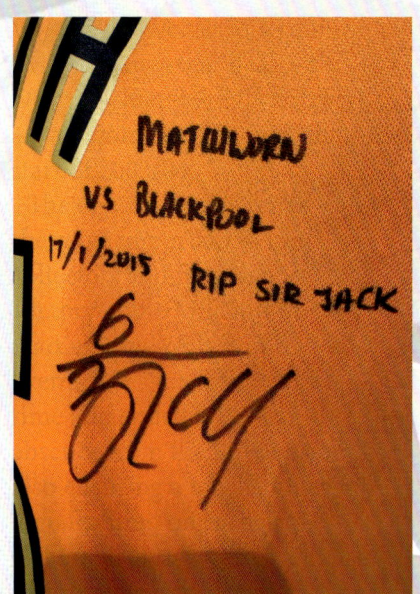

I was lucky enough to secure both captains' shirts from the game, Batth signing his with the match details and date, which is something I do like to see on very special occasions. He also supported the first book and charity fundraising, a true captain in every sense.

One thing to look out for with his shirts, because of his running style the armband rubbed against the shirt material causing bobbling, a sure sign it's been matchworn.

When it comes to stage managing big occasions with style and compassion no club does it better than Wolves. The news of Sir Jack Hayward's death at the age of 91 broke on the day of a home game against Fulham – a snow-hit FA Cup replay, his favourite competition.

Homage was paid that night but the main celebration of his astonishing life was held four days later during the Championship visit of Blackpool. Danny Batth was now captain of Wolves, just the sort of proud West Midlands boy Sir Jack loved to see make the first-team grade.

After finishing seventh the previous season, Kenny Jackett's men limped to a disappointing 14th this campaign which also saw Steve Morgan resign as chairman and put the club up for sale.

The shirt was typical modern-day Puma, traditional design, well constructed but some would argue a bit too orange in colour.

I have more disagreements about the shade of Wolves kits than any other subject, especially the recent 'yellow' ones. The fact is that the Old Gold colour spectrum ranges from yellow to rust, the latter being recognised as true Wolves Old Gold, as worn from 1930 to 1955 in the club's heyday. It was brought back in 2000-02 to celebrate the new millennium, but the majority didn't approve, being of the opinion that it was too dark.

The one bright spot of the season

was the signing of Conor Coady, though at the time he didn't look anything special at all. Signed from Huddersfield for an undisclosed fee believed to be £2 million, the shirt shown was worn on his debut, away at Blackburn Rovers.

Who would have thought back then that he would end his Wolves career on 273 games and be considered the best captain since Mike Bailey?

The first season under new owners Fosun heralded a change of manager, Walter Zenga replacing Kenny Jackett. Looking back at his previous record in management it was always going to be a risky appointment and so it proved with him lasting just 14 League games.

Paul Lambert was the next throw of the dice, taking over on 5th November, the fireworks coming in the FA Cup victories over Premier League Stoke and Liverpool, both away from home. Stearman wore this shirt at Anfield, heading home Costa's free

kick inside 53 seconds, Andreas Weimann adding the second before half-time.

Weimann also featured in the major kitman 'cock-up' of the season, wearing a shirt away at Brentford spelt 'Wiemann', again being captured by the camera. This time I was luckier in obtaining it for my collection.

There was an element of 'something old' and 'something new' about the home kit, pinstripes making a welcome return, although the new sponsor caused a fair amount of discontent amongst supporters.

It's fair to say that the first airing of the 'lime' shirt provoked a distinctly sour response, especially from first-team general manager Andrea Butti.

Wolves were unbeaten after six games when the shirt first appeared at Huddersfield, Butti being far from happy when he saw it in the dressing room. He insisted that the shirt "be put in the bin" and the "lucky" home kit used instead, which wasn't possible because the Football League and referee must be notified well in advance to avoid any possible kit clashes.

After the narrow 1-0 defeat Butti vowed it would never be worn

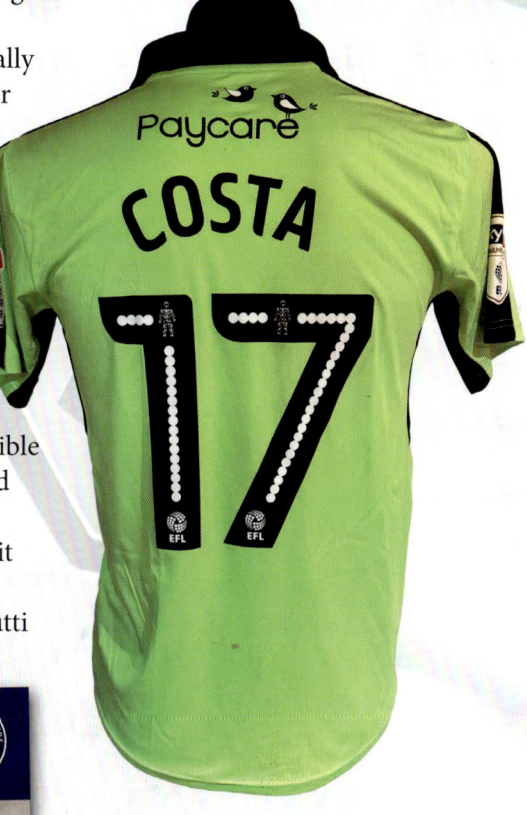

again, and it wasn't – at least until Butti was relieved of his position along with head coach Zenga.

Helder Costa wore this shirt when scoring a wonder goal away at QPR in December, Paul Lambert's first victory. Costa was the undoubted star of the season, winning every player and fan award, including Goal of the Season.

As for the 'lime' shirt? I tend to agree with Butti...

That was just one of many incredible moments that lit up Nuno and Neves' first season at the club, when we collected 53 points from a possible 69 at Molineux. Promotion as champions was achieved playing possession-based football with style and swagger, ending Wolves' six-year absence from the top division.

The shirt was beautiful. How could it possibly be judged otherwise after a season like that?

What a season! It's very rare in football that everything goes perfectly to plan, especially at Wolves, but this time it did just that.

The shocking news pre-season that Carl Ikeme had leukaemia served to galvanise the whole club, from new manager Nuno Espírito Santo to the fans.

The kit reveal saw a shirt launched into space, so it was fitting that some of the football played was out of this world. Neves wore this shirt at home versus Derby and scored possibly the best goal ever witnessed at Molineux, flicking the ball up slightly behind him before striking a stunning dipping volley into the top corner of the net.

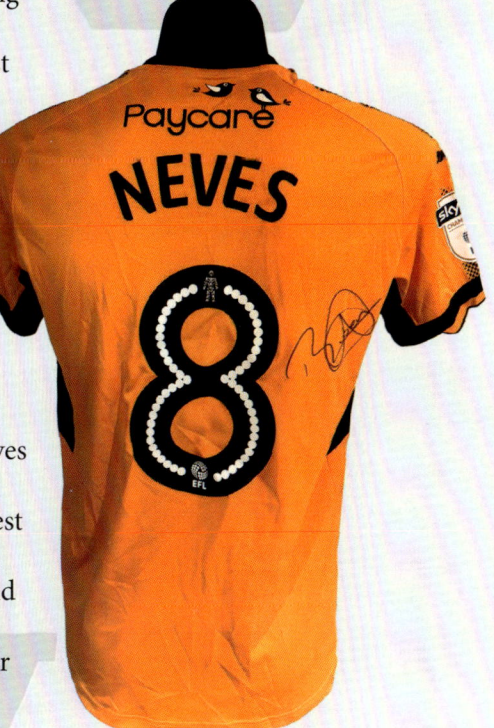

Another excellent kit from Puma, surprisingly only used three times, the blue third kit seeing more game time. The shirt was launched at the same time Rúben Neves signed. Perfection.

Back to black, always a good choice for a Wolves shirt, featuring a gold dotted asymmetric stripe, a really striking design touch which we will hopefully see again in the future. A sash-style shirt like this would also work superbly, perhaps even more so on a white kit.

This was worn in the epic victory at Bristol City, Danny Batth sent off early along with Nuno from the bench. With Wolves trailing 1-0, Douglas equalised from a free-kick then sent over another deep into added time for Ryan Bennett to head home, sparking unforgettable scenes in both the away end and the directors' box

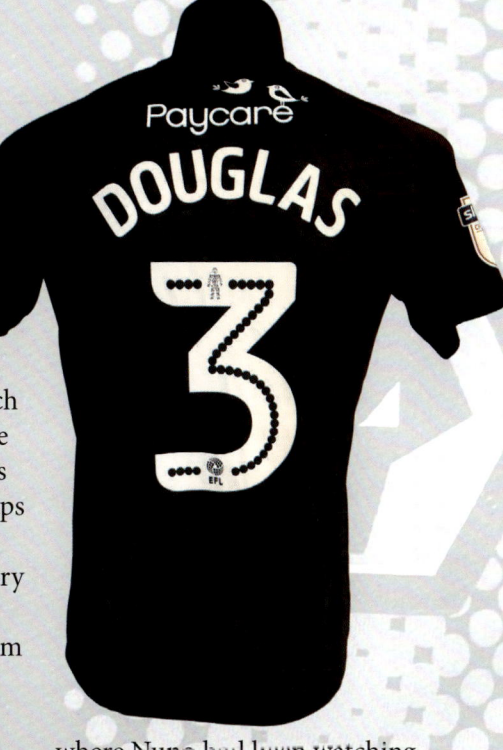

where Nuno had been watching. It was the sort of celebration we witnessed a lot that season, not least at Cardiff in another unbelievable away victory. Not so sure our old foe Neil Warnock enjoyed it, mind.

Barry Douglas was only here this one season, scoring five goals in addition to his 14 assists, joint highest in the Championship.

Did Wolves really need a third kit? Obviously not, but it completed an excellent trio of shirts for the champions elect.

Just 2000 of the limited edition were produced, although more were manufactured later due to such a high demand.

This was worn at Burton Albion by Diogo Jota, although Football League rules meant players had to have their surnames on the back rather than his preferred 'Diogo J.'

His real name would have been enough to give the kitman nightmares – Diogo José Teixeira da Silva.

In the four games the kit was worn, Wolves remained unbeaten,

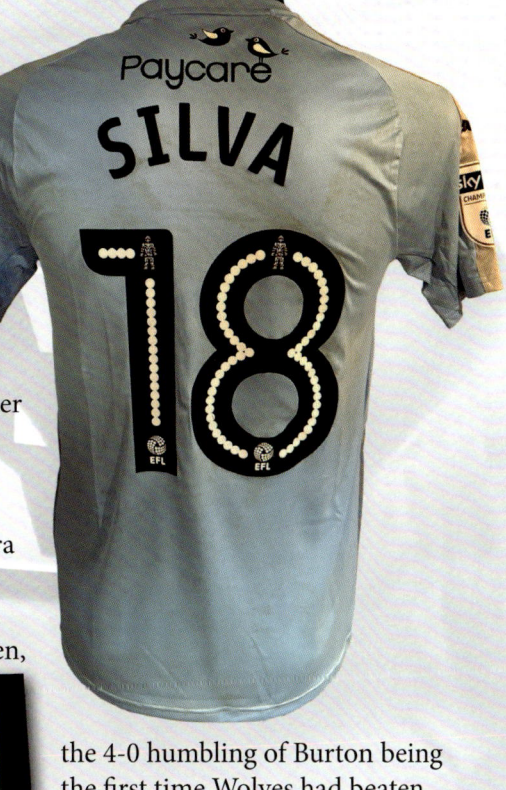

the 4-0 humbling of Burton being the first time Wolves had beaten the Brewers in our entire history (only having played them twice before, both times in the previous league season).

If you'd asked supporters at the Pirelli Stadium that afternoon to guess which player would go on to star for Liverpool in Champions League games, the vast majority would have answered Hélder Costa, but sadly the Angolan's career was wrecked by injuries.

clean, smart, classical look.

In truth, the football played that season was also a joy to behold, with stars aplenty, none more so than Benfica loanee Raúl Jiménez, who wore this shirt in the 2-1 victory over Manchester United in April 2019.

Wolves had arrived at the highest level in some style, finishing seventh and successfully qualifying for the Europa League, the almost perfect season only spoilt by a single game...

A Premier League patch on a Wolves shirt made by Adidas was music to the ears of shirt collectors and fans alike. Even better, the Money Shop sponsor was history, replaced by W88 – yes, an online gaming company, but one that, at least visually, brought back memories of 'Bully' and the Sherpa Van Trophy days.

'Old Gold, New Challenge' was the strapline behind the new kit colour, reminiscent of the yellow shade worn in the early 1900s. Despite a few moans, the shirt – which included a sleeve sponsor for the first time in the club's history – was very well received and is now highly prized for its

Wolves walking out at Wembley resplendent in a white Adidas away kit, just one game away from the FA Cup final, is some dream; but what transpired was a total nightmare.

The deepest cut of an otherwise remarkable season came in the FA Cup semi-final at Wembley, when Wolves let slip a 2-0 lead to Watford

to concede a last-gasp equaliser, and then go on to lose 3-2 in extra-time.

I vowed at the time this shirt worn by Rúben Neves on the day would never come out of storage, along with Conor's matchworn captain's armband and

a matchball from the game. Six years later, I'm still haunted by that Wembley defeat.

The fact that we qualified for Europe helped to lift the gloom, but in truth it felt like my last chance had gone to follow in dad's footsteps, singing 'Abide with Me' at the final of the greatest club competition in the world.

was a very proud moment for me.

Manchester City, West Ham and Newcastle were the other participants, Wolves easily beating the Magpies in their semi-final, wearing the new home shirt. The final against Manchester City was a close game, with the Molineux men eventually winning out 3-2 on penalties.

Over the years many sponsors have adorned the front of a Wolves shirt, but surely none better than Fosun in gold on the new black away shirt. And what a way to launch it, by lifting a trophy!

Wolves' pre-season plans were slightly more exotic than Ireland this time, having been invited to play in the prestigious Asia Trophy, a biennial competition inaugurated in 2003.

Held jointly in Shanghai and Nanjing, Fosun were keen to introduce the club to the Chinese public, and they achieved their aim in some style. A brand-new Megastore opened in Shanghai, and it was there that the excellent black away shirt was launched. Just around the corner was a pop-up exhibition displaying several Wolves shirts from years gone by, inspired by *They Wore the Shirt*, which

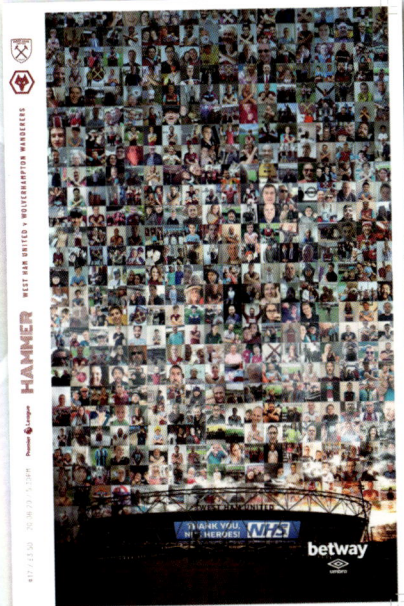

the last-eight defeat to eventual winners Sevilla.

The Premier League season was suspended on 13th March 2020 and resumed on 17th June, with all matches being played in empty grounds with no spectators. Wolves' first game back was a 2-0 victory at West Ham. João Moutinho wore the shirt featured, the only time that players' names have not appeared above their number. A very contentious shirt but also the rarest from a season no one will ever forget, for all the wrong reasons.

The season that promised everything, but ultimately ended in disappointment. Flying high in the Premier League and through to the final stages of the Europa League, surely nothing could derail the momentum Nuno's men were building.

Then Covid-19 struck, Wolves fans being blamed for a large outbreak locally after returning from the Espanyol game in Barcelona.

I'm convinced that without the break it caused, followed by the football played behind closed doors, Wolves would have stood a great chance of going further than

With Wolves doing well in both Premier League and Europa League, the black away shirt was used in both competitions to great effect.

Immediately, Willy Boly's winner right at the death in Beşiktaş springs to mind – wheeling away, Foundation sponsor across the front of the shirt, contrasted by yellow socks and shorts. These were rarely seen throughout the season as they were a totally different shade to the home shirt.

Wolves were back in all black for the Premier League clash when this shirt was worn, Raúl Jiménez scoring the decisive goal in a 2-1 win at Norwich.

Originally authentically smelly, having been soaked in sweat, with a chalk mark across the back, this shirt was air dried outdoors under cover before being bagged and labelled. This way, the shirt still retains that 'matchworn' odour but does not sweat in the bag causing the arm patches to peel off, a lesson learnt from experience.

Jiménez was at his peak and one of the best strikers in England, if not Europe, at this point; but his story was soon to take a calamitous turn for both player and club.

Early September saw Adidas launch the third Wolves shirt of the season, with a distinct Mexican flavour. Not only another superb offering but also a very clever marketing ploy by the club, with Jiménez at the height of popularity for both club and country.

Late October saw the shirt used twice in four days, firstly in the Europa League win in Bratislava then the 1-1 draw at Newcastle when this shirt was worn by captain Conor Coady.

It was also used in Espanyol, this time with the Foundation sponsor, this continual switching explaining why the club also had a boxful of shirts with nothing on the front.

In a season where games were coming thick and fast, it was perhaps inevitable that a kit mistake would occur at some point. When the team ran out at Watford all eyes were on Adama Traore or, more precisely, on the front of his shirt, which had no sponsor. All three of his shirts had been printed up without checking the front, a one-off mistake that will never be made again.

On the plus side, it did result in some free nationwide publicity for sponsors (of the rest of the players, at least), ManBetX!

Home v Beşiktaş – *Standard sponsor.*

Black Away v Braga – *Standard sponsor.*

Home worn in Torino – *Foundation sponsor.*

Black Away v Beşiktaş – *Foundation sponsor.*

Green Away v Espanyol – *Foundation sponsor.*

Green Away v Slovan Bratislava – *Standard sponsor.*

Home v Sevilla, quarter-final – *Standard sponsor with 'Thank You' above the badge.*

Home – *Foundation sponsor with 'Thank You'. Prepared for last eight tournament in Germany but never used.*

If the previous season wasn't disrupted enough by the Covid-19 pandemic, it was even worse this campaign, every Wolves home game being played behind closed doors with no fans in attendance until the very last. Throw in Raúl Jiménez fracturing his skull at Arsenal and Nuno leaving 'by mutual consent' after four years and it really was a season to forget.

This shirt was worn by Conor Coady at Leicester in November 2020, then auctioned for the Royal British Legion, just about the only way you could get an unwashed shirt under the strict restrictions put in place on player contact.

The shirt was possibly the worst home made by Adidas, an overcomplicated design combined with black arms not really working. Perhaps the strangest thing to happen because of the pandemic was the number of new collectors to the hobby. Lots of spare time with nothing to spend money on resulted in shirt prices rocketing, and four years later the market is still booming.

'Unique and urban design' was how Adidas described this shirt on release, only to be countered by online replies including: "This is offensive to anyone with taste," "No, just no," and "They'd have to pay me to wear that shirt."

I always try to be positive about everything, but the only plus about this kit is that it was only worn once. Even Nuno hated it! In a 4-0 drubbing by Liverpool, watched by just a handful of spectators in an echoing Anfield purged by Covid-19 restrictions, Neto's shirt was swapped post match.

This season's home kit was the most used in the Premier League, being worn 32 times – a testament to just how unpopular the away shirt was. Surely, it's odds-on favourite to win any future 'Wolves Worst Kit of All Time' poll.

After all the anticipation and excitement of finally having Adidas as kit supplier, it would have been a major disappointment had this been their final offering; but thankfully there was still one more to come.

shirts to good causes, so always keep an eye out on social media for local charity fundraisers where it's possible to add to your collection.

I think, overall, the Adidas Wolves kits were excellent, though definitely lifted in our memories by association with the successes of the first two years, finishing seventh in the Premier and reaching the last eight of the Europa League.

Those shirts with the Wolves font name and number, proudly displaying the Europa patch, will take some beating.

It was touch and go after the first two kits of the season, but Adidas went a long way towards redeeming themselves with the Portugal-inspired third kit. I especially liked the subtle white trim line.

#ReadyToBeBrave launched the shirt on Twitter (now X) but this stunner was never going to fail, especially with the sizeable Portuguese contingent wearing it, including João Moutinho, Rúben Neves, Rui Patricio, Pedro Neto and Nelson Semedo, who pulled on this very shirt away at Tottenham in May 2021.

Semedo is one of many players at the club who regularly donate their

New manager, new kit deal and new hope. Bruno Lage arrived with a reputation for being a master tactician while not perhaps the best at man management, the opposite of Nuno. The signing of Rayan Ait-Nouri and Jose Sa plus Hwang Hee-chan initially on loan gave even more reason for optimism.

Described as a 'Truly ground-breaking deal in Premier League football', Castore would now be producing all the on-field playing kit, with Wolves themselves manufacturing and distributing replica products under licence from Castore – in principle, an excellent deal for the club.

The big bonus for matchworn collectors was the player kits differing from the replicas, a first for Wolves in the Premier League.

Although they could still be purchased from the Megastore, the high cost reduced the amount of fakes until prices fell at the season's end. Amazing how many 'prepared' shirts crop up then.

Worn by Adama Traore in the FA Cup, this is an excellent shirt all round, complete with 'Beast' signature, wolf-eye font numbers and a '4' in the patch paying homage to Wolves' historic victories in the competition.

The Castore deal promised bespoke kit across all the ranges, and that's exactly what they supplied. This one has grown on me over time, ever since I got the initial thought of a train seat out of my mind.

Described as a 'unique design in anthracite, combined with yellow logos and black inserts on the shoulders and sides,' it really is very cleverly done.

All the professionals' shirts feature laser-cut detailing on the back and sides, helping greatly in the worst sweat zones, but the disrupted design does an excellent job of camouflaging them.

This shirt was match issued to Rúben Neves and swapped post match, which is how I've been able to obtain many of my

shirts over the years. Things have now changed for the better, and matchworn kit has never been so readily available, mainly thanks to the excellent Wolves Foundation, the club's official charity, and the many auctions they now hold, currently around seven or eight per season. Bidding is through MatchWornShirt, and the best bit of advice I can give is to wait until the actual shirt photos are put on before placing your bid. Many a good shirt has been ruined by a poorly placed signature.

JOAO MOUTINHO

2021/22 - Third - Poppy

166

The fact that I love a white away shirt is well documented; combine it with a unique poppy design and you're in special territory indeed.

This is simply a superb piece of kit. I would like to think it was based around the Manders 1988-90 shirts but, either way, it's tremendous. When launched, I never dreamt it could be bettered; but then along came the Remembrance games. I'd previously stopped collecting the poppy shirts when Wolves ditched the embroidery for transfers, but these were on another level.

I believe they were the brainchild of the current kit man who had them made as unique to the club, smaller than the standard poppy but with match details and date added. I'm lucky enough to own both Moutinho and Neves' away matchworns from the Crystal

Palace game plus Neves' prepared from the Everton home game. Moutinho's is featured here purely because it's not signed: why spoil a work of art with a signature?

Originally gifted to his hairdresser, Moutinho would kindly often give his shirts to people he knew well, including his favourite ice-cream man!

168

The season when it very nearly all went wrong. Bruno Lage was known to struggle with man management and decided he wanted respected senior professionals John Ruddy, Romain Saiss and captain Conor Coady moved on, mainly because they had played under Nuno and, he believed, had too much influence among the players.

The way he went about it, especially his treatment of Conor, meant it was only a matter of time before he lost the dressing room, and by early October he was gone.

Julen Lopetegui took over on 14th November, when he set about the task of steering the club away from relegation danger with the minimum of fuss. He was able to sign Dawson, Lemina, Sarabia and Gomes in the January

transfer window after more major investment from owners Fosun.

The shirt was another excellent offering from Castore, the black block on the lower back really looking the part when combined with the shorts.

Diego Costa wore this at Molineux versus Aston Villa, the damage to the front of the shirt coming about during an altercation with Tyrone Mings. Another superb unwashed shirt purchased from a Wolves Foundation auction.

170

'**G**eometric Molineux print inspired by the iconic girders and fixings of the Billy Wright Stand.' At least, that's what it said on the release statement for this shirt.

But surely a further bolt of inspiration also came from the popular away kit used between 1996-1998, when Steve Bull celebrated the 17th and penultimate hat-trick of his Wolves career versus Grimsby Town, a shirt featured earlier in the book.

Bull is an icon at Wolverhampton Wanderers, and there's only been one player who has since come even close to the adulation he enjoyed – Rúben Neves.

The fact he never turned against Bruno Lage, carrying on doing his job to the best of his ability, is testament to his attitude and professionalism.

Neves joined Wolves in 2017, winning the Football League Championship in his first season. He went on to make 253 appearances, scoring 30 goals – including possibly the best witnessed at Molineux against Derby County.

A captain who led by example, never giving less than 100 per cent whatever the circumstances, now rightly considered a modern-day Wolves legend.

'Dirtiest Ever Player' following several incidents that season, and in truth few could disagree with their judgment. His first headline for Wolves was for a gratuitous head butt in stoppage time at Brentford. The only shock was that it was the 34-year-old's first red card in the Premier League.

He fared better in the reverse fixture at Molineux, mind, getting on the scoresheet in the 2-0 victory. It was his solitary goal in 23 appearances, but Costa still played a big part in staving off relegation and helping rebuild the team spirit destroyed by Lage.

The Diego Costa I loved watching at Chelsea was brilliant and slightly unhinged in equal measure, my favourite Premier League striker of all time for those exact reasons. The man was pure box office.

Never in a million years did I imagine he would ever wear the Old Gold and Black – or, in this case, the Various Shades of Grey – for Wolves in the Premier League. He joined us in September 2022 and lasted until the end of the season. His best years were admittedly well behind him but he still exhibited just the same desire and hunger as ever.

In 2015 the *Daily Express* named Costa the Premier League's

174

Despite injuries to key players, he somehow managed to restore confidence within the whole group, team spirit comparable to the Nuno era and, after beating local rivals West Bromwich Albion in the FA Cup (Cunha's winning goal shirt below), cult status with the fans. The main shirt featured was matchworn by Mario Lemina,

Wolves' sixth consecutive season in the Premier League got off to a disastrous start, parting company with Julen Lopetegui by mutual agreement, Gary O'Neil being appointed head coach a day later.

With Neves, Costa, Moutinho, Traore, Collins, Jiménez, Nunes and the previously loaned-out Coady all leaving the club, Wolves were most pundits' favourites for relegation before a ball had been kicked. O'Neil had taken on an almost impossible job; but I'm now writing this just before Easter with Wolves safe from relegation and pushing for a European place.

my vote for Player of the Season.

It's rumoured to be Castore's final season as kit supplier. If so, they left the best home 'til last.

This one made me totally reconsider how I look at shirts, my initial response being 'strawberry mess'; but now I absolutely love it, the best of the three for this season, in my opinion.

I think sometimes you can have a preconceived idea of what doesn't make a good shirt, the 1992 'Tyre Track' shirt being a fine example. Throughout the book, I must stress the opinions expressed are mine and mine alone, I don't expect everyone to agree, and I'm looking forward to the feedback to gauge the thoughts of others.

The shirt featured was matchworn at Chelsea, where

Matheus Cunha scoring the club's first ever away hat-trick in the Premier League. Two weeks later it was worn again, this time at Tottenham, with Wolves winning 2-1. But defeat at Newcastle in early March put a stop to the 'lucky shirt' talk.

With his younger brother Noah signing on loan at the end of January, Mario successfully applied to the Premier League to change the name on his shirt, a first for Wolves at this level.

Another excellent kit from Castore: modern, stylish and great colour. I mentioned the uproar caused by changing the crest colour on the 2009/10 away shirt yet, 14 years on, you would get a similar reaction if it wasn't colour matched.

Moving forward, I would love to see two things – a 'whiteout' or 'blackout' Wolves kit and a return to Umbro as manufacturers, both for historical reasons and because of their recent catalogue for other clubs. If my wishlist were one day combined in a single shirt, I doubt it could ever be bettered!

Replica football kits are now

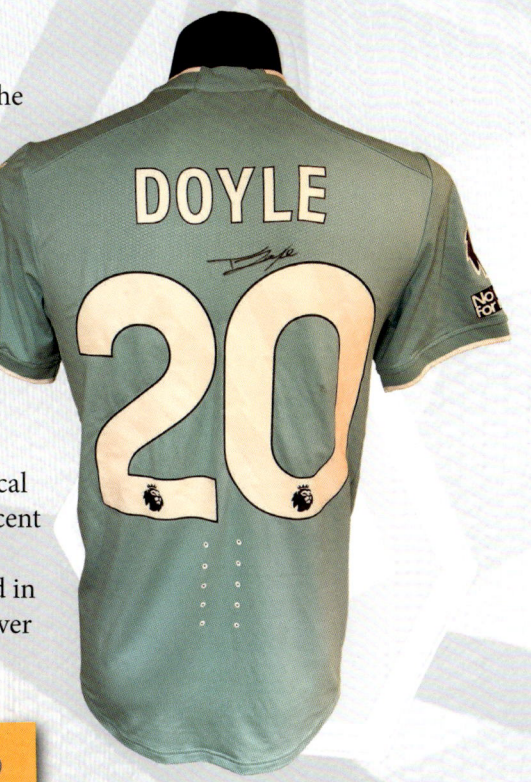

big business and can be excellent money spinners for clubs. To Wolves' credit they have embraced this over recent years and now sell a quality range of retro shirts, ideal if you can't afford the ever-spiralling price of the originals.

The shirt featured was worn by Tommy Doyle at Luton, another excellent shirt from the Wolves Foundation charity. It's never been easier to get Wolves matchworn shirts, but a warning: once you get one and the bug bites, your house might not be big enough!

May 1995: my first trip to Molineux with my newly acquired birthday money in hand and a desire to get my hands on my first Wolves shirt.

I fondly remember a walk around the stadium with my mum and dad in tow, the feeling of excitement and being overwhelmed by what I saw before we finally went into the old club shop. An instant love for the Old Gold and Black was just about to go up another level, and would later create a passion in my life not only for Wolves but also a love for football shirts. At the time, I didn't notice the finer details of

the shirt as I do now, but I did take in the Goodyear sponsor logo emblazoned on the front, together with the Nutmeg supplier brand. Who were Nutmeg? I didn't care. I just wanted that shirt on my back to wear proudly and to recreate my hero, Mr Steve Bull, down the local green. A fond memory is mum and dad's influence to buy the shirt a few sizes too big, so I would grow into it. I didn't care at the time – just take my money. The shirt still fits me now!

Fast forward to August 2012, my first day as an employee for my beloved club, and a chance to be more involved with the Wolves shirt than I ever thought possible. With a background in high-street retail, my initial role was to run the Megastore in the brand-new Stan Cullis Stand. As the club became more successful on the pitch I landed the role of retail operations manager, and in my ten-year spell with Wolves was lucky to be involved in many exciting projects with some fantastic people.

Did you like the pinstripe on the Puma shirt with a nod to 1982? What about hot pink goalkeeper shirts, or the European letters and numbers that became available to buy during that wonderful season under Nuno. All good memories, and now football shirt history.

Much of my input at the club was framed by my lifelong love for the shirt, and cherished memories of the replica kits us fans had bought in ever-increasing numbers over the years.

In the past, young kids always used to kick balls around in the street, up against a wall or 'jumpers for goalposts' whilst wearing a top that slightly resembled the colours of Wolves, and probably got their mum to sew on a club badge to heighten the illusion. But things are very different nowadays.

The most notable first replica for Wolves was back in the '70s, produced by Umbro. Well before my time, this is now one of the rarer targets for collectors, with the three Wolves on the chest. A few years later came my favourite shirt, with the beautiful 'Umbro diamond' trim running down the sleeves. Umbro are a manufacturer I'd love to see return one day; get the shirt right with a nod to the '70s and we'd all be on to a winner.

The Spall era saw Wolves start upping numbers, selling more of the Staw-sponsored shirts to fans than ever before, and the rise of the replica had really started. Bukta brought in a custom, self-

coloured fabric printed with the wolf's head which really gave the shirts a feel of being ours alone.

Another favourite set of shirts is the famous 1996 home and away 'wolf head' shirts by Puma. They were in the classic mid-'90s oversized style with the massive 'V' neck, shadow-printed wolf fabric and 'WW' sleeve taping. A truly bespoke kit, before the modern-day era of shirts based on supplier templates.

8th July 2017 was a day that stood out for me as a sign that we were going places as a club. A year on from the takeover, I remember working in the Megastore when news broke that we'd signed Rúben

Neves for a then club-record fee. Within 30 minutes the shop went from a regular season's soft kit launch to bedlam. Queues for shirt sales and shirt printing meant no lunchbreak, but what unbelievable

BUKTA

& WOLVES

■

FASHIONABULL

DESIRABULL

MEMORABULL

UNSTOPABULL

Bukta

support! The shirts were already selling out, on day one.

All businesses make retail decisions based on previous years' sales and other trading factors, and then budget accordingly. This is no different to ordering shirt volumes for a football club. We would commit x amount for the following season and split our buy across the two or three available kits.

We were often asked why we needed a third kit when no other side in our league wore gold and black. A third kit offered a choice in cup competitions in case we drew a club whose kit clashed; but the commercial possibilities soon became apparent when we started budgeting for a small run of a third colourway. Like a certain blue Puma shirt that was crazily launched online and instore at full time, with only 2,000 units available to buy – and then the inevitable question of 'when's the next delivery?'

Kit suppliers all work differently, but every one will want your volume numbers at least a year before the season starts – *some even two* – to ensure production timescales are met.

Here comes your first problem to try and solve, unfortunately with no crystal ball to predict the future: let's say last year you finished 15th in the league, and sold x amount before reducing the price to clear the surplus stock. So how many do

NUTMEG

Who are Nutmeg?

They are an American owned company who consistently produce quality garments for the licenced sportswear trade.

Formerly known as 'Kick', the company has created innovative designs for some of the biggest names in world sport: Chicago Bulls, L.A. Raiders, New York Yankees, and Bayern Munich to name a few.

Nutmeg are now proud to focus this expertise on Wolverhampton Wanderers F.C. by supplying the team kit, as well as continuing with their range of exciting fanwear.

The partnership between Wolves and Nutmeg will bring success both on and off the pitch.

Stand out from the crowd!

we order for the season after next? Wait a minute, though – we're playing good football, and with heavy player investment we can dream of a promotion push. The shirts are selling out, and fans are asking when we'll be getting more stock... but the answer is we won't, because we ordered this season's shirts two years ago, when there was no sign demand might outstrip supply! It's frustrating for all parties, but it isn't possible to 'simply' order some more.

Once the season

has started and the new shirts have been on sale for a couple of weeks, we then have to sit down to select options for the year after next. Working with the big names, you don't get much of a say at all: you normally only get the choice of a couple of options. These are template shirts that are then customised into the new season's shirt, so a club crest and sponsor will be added. These all need to be agreed and signed off so that the factories can plot a time slot to produce the shirts.

Working with other departments, you're awaiting the call to say the main sponsor has been agreed and a logo designed, so the shirt can go into production. If it hasn't yet been agreed, then the shirt is manufactured and the logo added later, normally when they land in

Wolves

ClubShop

HOME TOP OFFER!

ADULTS £25
YOUTHS £22
CHILDS £20

MOBILE PHONE ACCESSORI

AVAILABLE AT THE MOLINEUX, MANDER CENTRE, DUDLEY STREET & THE MERRY HILL CLUB SHOPS the UK. But that's a lot of work on its own, making sure that it's the correct size and compliant with governing bodies, and that the sponsor is happy with final designs. Like all clubs, you strive to get the best financial deal for commercial reasons, but the knock-on has a very real impact.

June comes round fast, and there's pressure from fans for the shirts to be released or announced on social media. It isn't easy, if shirts are being printed up day and night to get them finished. Just before the players depart for holidays, a

confidential photoshoot is called and the new kits are pictured from samples. Sometimes the shirts are Photoshopped after the sponsor has been agreed, if it hasn't been signed off in time. So that's done, artwork all created, socials done, launch story ready and a date is selected for launch... But did someone mention a sleeve sponsor? Looks like it should be out late July!

Working with certain suppliers, you may get more of a free rein, being presented with designs and the chance to add in your own bespoke, unique finesse touches, and also to control the exact colour.

So it's not orange... it's gold.

Maybe some would argue it's not Old Gold but, even to this day, there's much healthy debate around this vital question! I remember when the colour change happened in 2018. We had to run tests to make sure it didn't change

tone under the floodlights or when it rained, just two of the countless details checked every year to ensure the shirt comes out absolutely right.

The future of our football shirts will always cause debate and divide opinions, and long may this continue. It normally signifies the start of the season is coming.

I personally believe we may see a change in the near future, where more clubs create and produce shirts in-house, claiming the current suppliers' cut to generate maximum possible profit. Indeed, Wolves created their own Molineux brand back in the '90s when a kit supplier deal wasn't agreed, and then did likewise with WWFC in the early 2000s.

As has apparently been discussed at several clubs, complete design and manufacturing control of the

shirt would then make available further commercial 'real estate' on the lucrative front of the shirt – perfect for, let's say, a 'club badge' or 'kit' sponsor? Who knows? It's only my opinion; only time will tell and, as I've noted before, no one has a crystal ball...

1977-79 – Umbro change shirt

Discovered on a well-known shirt-sale website advertised as a replica for under £100!

Small holes in the back due to the kitman removing the number to reuse, common practice at the time.

Part of the Carl Falconer collection.

1982/83 – Umbro change shirt

The first time a sponsor appeared on the Wolves shirt.

Discovered in New Zealand and mainly worn by Tim Flowers alongside John Burridge.

Part of the Carl Falconer collection.

**1988 – Spall
Sherpa Van Trophy**

Issued to Mark Kendall and worn for the pre-final photocall, but he preferred wearing his favourite brand of shirt during the game.

Post-match swap with his friend and Burnley goalkeeper Chris Pearce, who kept it for 33 years.

Part of the Carl Falconer collection.

1992/93 – Molineux home

What a shirt! With the '90s club and festival scene in full flow, you could imagine that the designer enjoyed a good rave!

Years ahead of its time, and now rightly considered a classic.

Worn by Mike Stowell, and part of the Carl Falconer collection.

1994/95 – Nutmeg home
FA Cup fourth-round replay

Worn by Paul Jones in that incredible game against Sheffield Wednesday. 1-1 after extra-time and 3-0 down in the penalty shoot-out, Wolves pulled it back to 3-3 before Jones made his second save, Goodman then scoring to clinch it 4-3.

   Part of the Carl Falconer collection.

2002/03 – Admiral
First Division Play-off final

Embroidered in readiness for the final with Sheffield United in Cardiff. 24 hours before the game it was pointed out that Matt Murray's shirt would clash with the referee's. Embroidered patches were rushed to the team hotel and hand sewn on to the blue shirts that were used!

   Part of the Carl Falconer collection.

2017/18 – Puma change shirt

A white keeper shirt would have been unimaginable in the past, yet this was Wolves' second in consecutive seasons. Matchworn by John Ruddy in the first half at Burton Albion in the Championship-winning season – muddy and unwashed.

2019/20 – Adidas Europa League change shirt

Due to advertising restrictions in Turkey, the Foundation sponsor replaced ManBetX for the Besiktas game. To follow suit, the same sponsor was also used in Torino and Espanyol.

Issued to John Ruddy.

1993/94 – Molineux

1994-96 – Nutmeg

1994/95 – Second

1995/96 – Second

1996-98 – Puma

1996-98 – Second

1998-2000 – Puma

1999/2000 – Puma

2000/01 – Second

2000-02 – Wolves Leisure

2001/02 – Second

2002-04 – Admiral

2002/03 – Play-off

2003/04 – Second

2004/05 – Third

2004/05 – Second

2004/05 – Le Coq Sportif

2005/06 – Le Coq Sportif

2005/06 – Second

2006/07 – Second

2006/07 – Le Coq Sportif

2006/07 – Third

2007/08 – Le Coq Sportif

2007/08 – Second

2008/09 – Le Coq Sportif

2008/09 – Second

2009/10 – Le Coq Sportif

2009/10 – Second

2010/11 – Burrda

2010/11 – Second

2011/12 –
Second

2011/12 – Burrda

2011/12 –
Third

2012/13 – Second

2012/13 – Burrda

2012/13 – Third

2013/14 – Third

2013/14 – Puma

2013/14 – Second

2014/15 – Change

2014/15 – Puma

2014/15 – Change

2015/16 – Puma

2015/16 – Second

2015/16 – Third

2016/17 – Puma

2016/17 – Second

2016/17 – Third

2017/18 – Change

2017/18 – Puma

2017/18 – Change

2018/19 – Change

2018/19 – Adidas

2018/19 – Change

2019/20 – Change

2019/20 – Adidas

2019/20 – Change

2020/21 – Change

2020/21 – Change

2020/21 – Adidas

2021/22 – Castore

2021/22 – Change

2021/22 – Change

2022/23 – Castore

2022/23 – Change

2022/23 – Change

2023/24 – Castore

2023/24 – Change

2023/24 – Change

2024/25 – Sudu

2024/25 – Change

2024/25 – Change

Author

Steve Plant's journey into matchworn collecting didn't begin until 2009 but in the 15 years that have followed he's put together a stunning collection of shirts and built his own museum full of rare memorabilia, while also managing to raise over £250,000 for charity under the 'They Wore the Shirt' banner.

When not in his beloved museum, you will most likely find him over Kinver Edge with his Labradors Lilly, Poppy and Daisy – like Steve, they are all Plants!

Acknowledgements

Without the support of my loving wife Andrea and network of friends, none of this would have been possible.

Simon Shakeshaft and more recently Neville Evans helped immensely, not least in helping me gain credibility amongst my fellow collectors, and thanks to Gary and Derek at Conker Editions for their help in delivering exactly the book I visualised.

Thanks to the legend that is Greg Elliott for building my dream museum and constantly making me laugh, to Pottsy for always having my back, to Shaun and Foz for going above and beyond, and to Mark Bullock for being there when I need advice and a full English breakfast!

Special mention to Steve Saul for putting our dinners together, my apprentice George Brown, Jon and Rich from the Wolves Facebook group, Carl Falconer, Jason Guy, Lawson Slater and my inspiration Neil Taylor.

Finally a special mention to Greg's late wife Claire – intelligent, inspirational, 'one of the boys', forever loved and missed by all who knew her x

Photo Credits

With thanks to Michael Petalengro for the 'Bully' car park image, Jim Mayer, and the Bagnall family for all their help and support of 'They Wore the Shirt'. Image on page 157: Simon Kimber.

Teamwork...

Chris Worrall | Leigh Billings | Matt Cleverly | Neil Simpson

Kieran, Ted & Conor Newey | Steve Mohammed | Andrew Jebb

Hong Trang Nguyen | Richard Shearman | Allan Lee Kronenbach

Stefan Hales-Józefczyk | Jon Lawton | Douglas John Pearl

Tony Malpass | Keith Bickley | Peter Kane | Jake Perry

Tom Daniels | Ian Hastings | Warwick Nash | Gavin Haigh

Paul Davies | Harrison Turner | Lewis Turner | Jonathan Russell

Stevie Bernard | Nigel O'Connor | Mitchell Aspland | Adam Lake

David Collins | Matthew Dean | Louis Nicholls | Glen Baldwin

Russell Beddoe | Steven Green | Matthew Bell | Odin Henrikssen

George Fabian | Adrian Mann | Louis Johnson BEM

James Bateman | Craig Lewis Williams | Sophie Drayton

Callum Wright | Connor Wright | Jonathan Moorby | Chris Brown

Chris Clarke | Jamie Clarke | Steve Knowles | Anthony Butler

Daniel Hughes | Cyril Farrow | Carl & Alison Ackasovs

Josh Moorby | Keith Moorby | Dave Foster | Barrie Webb

Aaron Davies | Brett Turner | Peter & Romy Waller

Bohdi Shields | Jon Haywood | Steve Harper

David Lowe | Jon - @wolves_shirts

Jonathan Pålsson | Robert Stanley

Alan John Winmill | Royston Newey

Mark Rigby | Edward Hon-Sing Wong

Carl Jackson | Paul Allen | Bill Garner

Steve Robinson | David Jones

Dean Griffiths | Tim Rouse

Jake Rouse | Colin Rouse | David Jones

Kevin Greenfield | Michael Sniffer Turner

Nav (asianwolf) & June Phokela | Robert Knight | Tom Huxley
Zak Hughes | Brian Whybrow (Dad) | Steve YamYam Jones
Martin Lacey | Peter Lacey | Stu Hall | Richard Griffiths
Nigel O'Connor | Lewis Eades | Justin Greenstone | John Reynolds
Carl Hickman | Paul Hickman | Carles Mir Dillet | Anwar Ahmed
Lee Graham Wycherley | John Renshaw | James Collier
Chris Collier | Alli Collier | Sharon Dimmer | Darren Roberts
Happy Birthday Alan May (82) | Louis Turner | Mave the Rave
Andrew Deakin | Dale Race | Christian Bastable | Tim Mitchell
Conan Hipwell | Stu Parry | Daron Broome | Ros Pedley
John Bleach | John Moreton | John Clarke | Sotirios Korologos
Martyn Clewes | Ellis Bird | Mario Santangelo | Isla-Rose Key
David Roberts | Alex Tudor | Mike Peppiatt RIP | Kieron Brown
Mark Robert Newman | Christopher Driver | Mark Smith
Maurice Harvey | Toni Ragno | Jack Ellis | Adam Hughes
Jim Webb | Debbie Nicholls | Peter Aston | James Aston
Stephen Taylor | Olivia & Jonas Guy | Mark Winzor
Mat Winzor | Peter Richardson | Arthur Bullock
Jolene Bullock | Brad Bullock
ARC Electrical UK Services Limited
Adam Checketts | Steve & Pete Carvell
Ben & Bella Hawthorn | Lee Morris
Neil Maton | Nic Bullock | Trent Lay
Steve Saul | Craig Edwards
Joel Humpage | Brad Wilkinson
Nigel Hilliam | Stu and Lisa Clowes
Nick Jones | Nicholas Morris
Scott & Christina Jacobson | Micheal Hawthorn
Suzanne & Lissy Waterhouse & Brian Woodall
- remembering Janice Lee | Pam & John Causer
Clifford Roy Rigby | Matt Geal | Joe Ordidge

Rosey Pellington | Kev Wallsgrove | Chance Bowen | Joe Crisp
David Fleming | Daron Broome | Steve Mills
Justin Leadbetter | Aaron Hickman | Jeff Milham
Rob Morris | Robert Orchard | Paul Hickman
Rya Rutter | Neil Clapp | Pip Aldridge
Alfred Geoffrey | Steve Plant
Ian Clark | Mark (Alf) Holford -
Florida Wolves | Albie Arlo Mylo
Rob Cross | Marco Mozzachiodi
Carl Watson-Wood
Lawson Slater - in memory
of my good friend and fellow
Wolves fan Tito Jackson